The Spirit of Ned

BERT O'FLANNAGAN

DEDICATION

For

The Relations of

Ned and Dan

Copyright

©2015 Bert O'Flannagan

The moral right of Bert O'Flannagan to be identified as the Author of the work has been asserted by them in accordance with the Copyright, Designs and Patents Act 1988. All rights reserved. No part of this book may be used or reproduced by any means, graphic, electronic, or mechanical, including photocopying, recording, taping or by any information storage retrieval system without the written permission of the publisher except in the case of brief quotations embodied in critical articles and reviews.

National Library of Australia Cataloguing-in-Publication entry

Creator:	O'Flannagan, Bert, author.
Title:	The spirit of Ned / Bert O'Flannagan.
ISBN:	9780994282705 (paperback)
Subjects:	O'Flannagan, Bert--Authorship.
	Creative writing.
Dewey Number:	A823.4

Publishing Consultants: Pickawoowoo Publishing Group

Cover: Pickawoowoo Publishing Group - Marion O'Callaghan

Book Interior: Ned Kelly gold coin picture courtesy of Downies PL

Back Cover Portrait, Ned Kelly: Courtesy of State Library of Victoria Picture Collection. Creator William J. Burman H96.160-200

Printed & Channel Distribution

Lightning Source | Ingram (USA/UK/EUROPE/AUS)

ACKNOWLEDGEMENTS

It is with great respect that I Salute, Acknowledge, and thank the following fine Australian Authors and Historians.

Gary J Dean F.A.I.H.A. and Dagmar Balcarek F.A.I.H.A. for, their Historical Novel "ELLEN KELLY" and their Historical Novel "NED and the others".

Not only did their Novels fill my mind with facts but did inspire me to do what I suppose I always wanted to do = Write.

Thank you, and bless you both.

Gary and Dagmar have already Acknowledged Ian Jones for his book "NED KELLY a short life".

I also acknowledge Ian Jones, as a Guru of Kelly history and a great Author.

The above mentioned Authors are True Aussies.

The "Birth" of the "Aussie Digger" is said to have started in the year of 1854, when the gold miners of Victoria, Australia, led by a man named Peter Lalor, "took a stand" against the Government and the harsh laws that they had enforced by a cruel Constabulary. The ever increasing cost of Miners licences was too much, and the Police seemed to enjoy beating and locking up those miners who, unless they were some of the lucky few that found gold, could not pay these fees.

The "Stand" that they took is now a piece of Australian history. It is known as "The Eureka Stockade".

At about the same time, another leader of men was born into this land where the oppressive Government and Constabulary were to make his and his Family's life one of constant hounding. Like Peter Lalor this new born was destined to become a part of Australian history and folklore, because when he was man enough, "he took a stand," which cost him his life. Ned Kelly's stand at Glenrowan helped force a Royal Commission into the entire Victorian Police Force, and instigated the modern day Force. Ned Kelly has been labelled by some as a murderer, and by some as a hero. As you read on you may come to the conclusion that in the times that he lived in, and the way he was persecuted, that he had no choice. He was Ned Kelly.

FORWARD

If in my writing of this book my words appear to be telling the life of Ned Kelly in a different way to other books, or if some may believe that some of what my pen has been guided to write, may not be the actual facts, then I cannot apologise. I can only say that how do we or anyone write anything with the knowledge that what they write are the actual happenings? Remembering that the supposed actual facts were first written by somebody, then in our minds it will always come back to what we believe or is believable.

The Indigenous Australians have the ability to through their minds, pass on history and folklore from generation to generation. The human mind is a marvellous piece of machinery.

I ask you to open your mind and take in these writings that I somehow have been guided to scribble out. I named this book as such, because each time I picked up a pen my arm was in fact directed what to write, and I found it almost impossible to stop.

CONTENTS

Dedication	iii
Copyright	iv
Acknowledgements	v
Forward	vi
Contents	vii
Prelude	ix
Chapter One - As a Child	1
Chapter Two - I had to grow up	3
Chapter Three - I am the apprentice	6
Chapter Four - Now a partner	8
Chapter Five - Lookout Neddie	11
Chapter Six - A score is settled	16
Chapter Seven - I meets Fitzpatrick	22
Chapter Eight - We are the Kelly Gang	26
Chapter Nine - They come to Stringybark	32
Chapter Ten - We Run We Hide	38
Chapter Eleven - EUROA	44
Chapter Twelve - Desperate Men	49
Chapter Thirteen - Jerilderie is ours	52
Chapter Fourteen - The Letter	62
Chapter Fifteen - I Can Take No More	77
Chapter Sixteen - Me Final Plan	82
Chapter Seventeen - 'Shindig at Glenrowan'	87
Chapter Eighteen - Thomas Curnow	91
Chapter Nineteen - It's What We Are Here For	95
Chapter Twenty - Goodbye Me Brother	98

Chapter Twenty One - Game or Mad?	100
Chapter Twenty Two - They Have Me	103
Chapter Twenty Three - Am I Dead?	107
Chapter Twenty Four - My Country No More	109
Chapter Twenty Five - I Am Still Ned	113
Chapter Twenty six - Pentridge Again	115
Chapter Twenty Seven - Trial or Event?	119
Chapter Twenty Eight - "May the Lord Have Mercy on Your Soul."	121
Chapter Twenty Nine - Me Last Days	124
Chapter Thirty - Such Is Life	127
Bibliography	130

PRELUDE

I was given life in eighteen fifty four

Born to Ellen and John who married in eighteen fifty. Me mother eloped cause her dad picked John to be a failure, so he took his chances and took her to Melbourne very swiftly. Me mother was an Irish lady named Quinn and me dad a Tipperary convict named Kelly. It seemed that at first me dad didn't fit in, but he worked hard, cause he loved his Nellie.

Edward. Ned, they named me. I was brought up in harsh times but we all stuck together as a Kelly family. We were hounded and persecuted by those English swine.

Much has been written of me and about me, not all of it true, so I have through this medium, been given this chance to tell my story as it was and can only be. So read this, and as you do let your mind not dwell.

CHAPTER ONE

As a Child

I remember as a child how me mum used to tell us about her life in Ireland. She talked a lot about her grandparents who used to live with them. How her grandfather Patrick Quinn carved a wooden doll for each of the girls, and they used to dress them up and play until the boys would run through and spoil their game. She said her grandmother Mary was always singing, that was until her father told them of his plan to go to Australia. Me mother remembered her grandfather pleading with her father not to go to the far off land. She said her father said that he could not make a living off this land and in these conditions any more, and added that he was going to Australia as a bounty migrant so things would be easier.

Me mother used to cry as she told us of their last night in Ireland. She said even her father who was not really religious knelt between his parents and everyone said the Lord's Prayer.

"ARnathairataarneamg, go naofard'ainm; go g taga do rioch; go ndeantardothoilorantalamh ma a niteararneamh …".

She said nobody slept that last night in Ireland. She told us it was in the year 1841 that they arrived in this country of promise. They had travelled in the ship "The England" and were dropped off in Melbourne. It had taken 104 days to get to where her father hoped to give them a better life.

At about the same time Sean Caellaigh, Irish for John Kelly, was tried and found guilty of stealing two pigs and was sentenced to seven years in the penal colony on Van Diemans land. Me mother tells me that her father were probably right about making a better living, though she said it were very hard for a start. They had to live in a tent, and her father, me Grandfather James Quinn found work where he could. He was a woodcutter, a builder's labourer and did many odd jobs to make a living. Money was tight but finally they had enough to rent land and start a dairy farm in Brunswick.

After a few years they moved to a better farm in Broadmeadows and ma's brothers, Patrick and John, were now old enough to work with their father. Ma's mother gave birth to her last child in Melbourne, who was her tenth child.

Ma told me how she had met me dad at a dance, and how he had introduced himself as Red Kelly. Ma asked him his real name and told it was John or Sean in Irish. Ma decided to call him Sean. He then told her he had been sent out as a convict and had once received the lash.

Me mother and her Sean eloped and were married in St Francis Roman Catholic Church in Melbourne on the eighteenth of November eighteen fifty.

Her father gave them a small piece of land on the banks of the Merri Creek where they built their first home. Ma told me that in February eighteen fifty one, a bushfire burnt their house down and they had to build another one.

After a while her Sean got the gold fever and off he went to Bendigo where he found enough gold to pay for the new house and buy some horses and cattle. She told us how in 1853 they had saved enough money to buy their own farm in Beveridge where I was born on 28 December 1854.

Me mother told us how her Sean started drinking and not working as much and eventually they had to sell their farm. Her husband, me dad, continued to drink and bought and sold several more farms and finally moved to Avenel in 1864.

This I can remember, and I remember going to school in Avenel where Mr Wilson Brown gave me a pass in the three 'Rs'; reading, riting and rithmetic. Father O'Hea was the Catholic priest there and he visited us on many occasions. I recall me dad being arrested for stealing a calf which upset me Ma. Very clearly I remembers the arrival of me sister Grace in 1865 to join Anne, Maggie, James, Dan, Kate and me.

CHAPTER TWO

I had to grow up

With me dad locked up I had so much work to do around our farm as well as chopping the firewood and carting all our water up a steep hill to our house so Ma tells me I had better leave school. Mr Wilson Brown came to our house shortly after I left and told Ma that he thought I was a smart student and a pleasure to teach and he would like me to carry on with schooling. Ma gives him a cup of tea and thanks him for his concern and for coming all the way to try to help me, she then says that our family is very poor and with me dad in prison, there is no other way for the farm work to be done.

All the heavy work I has to do, I enjoys, and it builds me muscles up and I soon had to put them to use as some of the bigger boys around Avenel starts teasing me about me dad being in gaol. I had several fights because of this and I soon learnt to defend meself.

These very muscles helped me rescue a seven year old lad from drowning. His name was Dick Shelton, who had decided to cross the swollen Hughes Creek on a red gum tree that had fallen over the creek. I watched as he made his way across, and I thought for all money he was going to make it until that is he lost his straw hat which became stuck in the branches of the tree. Dick edges his way out towards his hat, and suddenly I hears a loud crack and the branch breaks away from the main tree. Dick screams as he falls into the swirling water. I remember diving in without thinking and swimming out to the drowning boy.

THE SPIRIT OF NED

I grabs him by the shirt collar and manages to get his head out of the water and I am pleased when he coughs up water. At least he is still alive I thinks. I tries to swim towards the bank but could not as the current was too strong. After struggling for a while, I felt a calmness sort of come over me and I realized it was no good fighting against the current, so still hanging on to the young lad, I lets the current wash us downstream and we were washed ashore.

We both lay there on the muddy bank fighting for air for quite a while, and then I took Dick to his parents at the hotel they owned. By this time there is a crowd of people and someone must have run ahead and told Dick Shelton's father, because he comes out and thanks me, and tells the crowd that 'Ned Kelly has just saved our son from drowning.'

He then gets three cheers from the onlookers, then Mr Shelton presents me with a fine green sash made of silk. This has gold fringes on each end, and I proudly wore it everywhere after that. Little did I know then how this sash would later on play an important part in Dan and my lives?

I had previously met Mr Shelton as I had found his lost horse for which he had given me a reward of ten shillings which I gave to me ma. Me dad 'Red Kelly' died in eighteen sixty six. Only a week after me Aunty Margaret's wedding to Patrick Quinn, the Dubliner. I helped me Ma attend me dad in his last days and I can still hear his final words as he whispered to me, 'Look after your Ma Ned.'

Ma asked me to leave her alone with him and I did as she wished. It was two days after Christmas, and one day before me twelfth birthday that me dad died. I remember how upset me Ma was, and I looked after her more than ever and became even closer to her. After me dad's funeral everyone came to our house. There were the Quinn's, the Kelly's, the Lloyds and the Millers. Ma got upset that day when me aunties, Kate and Jane started to complain about their husbands being in prison.

I felt that they had no right to complain in front of Ma on this sad day, so I asked them to stop it. They both said I was a rude child, but me Ma jumped up and told loudly that, 'Ned is no longer a child; he is now the man of the house.' I felt about twenty feet tall and much older than my twelve years.

At this wake, me uncles were all drinking a lot and soon started quarrelling and Uncle Jimmy was looking for a fight. 'Get out of here,' yells me Ma, and then without thinking I jumps up stands by her side and snarled, 'Leave Ma alone.' All was quiet for a moment then everyone left. Ma looks at me standing there with me fists clenched and she says, 'Thank you Neddie.'

Things started to happen around this time, and I think it was about this time I started to realize there was the rich and the poor. Money was very scarce for us poor people, so the temptation was there to take a little off the rich pastoralists who indeed thought they were better than us.

I remembers me Brother Dan got his name in the police gazette saying he was a suspect horse thief. Dan was only five at the time. Me Ma said the traps were aiming to put us all in prison and that our family had no hope while we were living in Avenel.

Soon after we moved to Greta near Glenrowan and lived with me aunties, Kate and Jane whose husbands, Jack and Tom Lloyd were serving five years in Pentridge for cattle stealing. I helped run their little farm which made just enough money for us all to live on.

One night me dad's brother, James who had just been released from gaol, paid us an unexpected visit. He was quite drunk and soon started making advances towards Aunty Kate. Me other aunty, Jane, picked up a gin bottle and broke it over his head, and I helped throw him out.

In the early hours of the morning Aunty Kate woke us all up yelling, 'Fire.' Fire there was. Drunken Uncle James had set fire to the house and we were lucky to get out and save most of the contents. Next day Uncle James was found hiding in the shoemaker's shop and was arrested, tried and sentenced to hang.

This was later changed to fifteen years gaol. This was the first time I had seen the judge they called hanging Barry, but it was destined not to be the last. After a while Ma got a little farm at Eleven Mile Creek and we moved there to live. I worked hard and time went fast in Greta.

CHAPTER THREE

I am the apprentice

I am now fourteen and being the man of the house began to fear no one as I was quite big for me age and learned how to fight from necessity. I grew to love horses and would ride for hours on end. Little did I know that I was soon to be taught to be an expert horseman by the best bushman round?

I woke one night to the sound of someone knocking loudly on our door, so I grabs me pistol and watches as Ma let in a well-dressed stranger. He wore handmade riding boots, flashy clothes and hanging from his vest pocket was an expensive looking watch. 'Allow me to introduce myself Mrs Kelly,' he said. 'I'm Harry Power, your humble servant ma 'mm.'

Ma listened as the confident man told her how he had met the Lloyds in Pentridge Gaol and that Tom would be coming home soon. He asked Ma if he could stay for a few days and Ma said it would be alright. He by now, had not even looked at me but then he says still without even glancing at me, 'You must be Ned, and if you are going to point that pistol at me any longer young man then you had better be prepared to use it.' He grins at me and slowly opens his jacket and I sees a bone handled pistol aimed straight at me. Harry Powers then laughs and puts his gun away and gestures for me to do the same. We seemed to hit it off and we talked for hours that night.

He produced a copy of the police gazette from Avenel which was printed just after we moved away. It read, "Edward Kelly, a Victorian native, aged fourteen years, five feet four or five inches high, stout build, brown hair, light grey eyes, smooth face, worn black jumper, moleskin trousers, cloth cap and bluchers."

'Apparently a neighbour dobbed you in Ned.' I asks him what for and he says the man reckons you pinched his horse lad. He laughs and I joins in when he adds, 'Now they've surely made a mistake there eh, anyone can see you're closer to six foot tall.' I was sorry to see him leave but he comes back after a few weeks, and very often after. I got to know him and he taught me a lot about horses. How to be able to approach even a wild one. Mostly he taught me to ride and hide in the thick bush, something that would help me later on.

I sort of joined up with Harry, as he insisted I call him. He was of course the famous bushranger and Ma warned me that no good would come of it. I did not listen to me Ma and held Harry's horse for him while he stuck up stages. He then started stealing horses, mainly from up Mansfield way as there were many rich farmers there with good horses. I guess I became his apprentice, and this went on for many months and I learned a lot, some of which Ma said would get me into trouble. She was right. I recall one day Harry and I were on a business trip up Mansfield way, on Mount Batty Station where real good horses were bred, when the station owner Dr Rowe and a few of his workmen fired upon us. I reckon I beat Harry back by nearly a mile that day.

I was still only fourteen when I was arrested and had to spend a week in gaol waiting for charges to be laid. The traps charged me with highway robbery. This was thrown out of court because no witnesses could recognize me. I am nearing fifteen now and its October 1869. I was tending me horses at home when a Chinaman named Ah Fook approaches our house. Me Sister Anne was sitting outside and Ah Fook says to her, 'Can I have water please?' Anne was very nervous but gave the grubby man a drink. He spits out at me sister and yells at her, 'water no good.' I ran over and told him to go away, but no, instead he swings his bamboo stick at me head. Then seeing how big I was and how easily I dodged his feeble blows he runs off. I never knew what he was really after that day, but the next day the traps come out and arrests me again. The Chinaman, through an interpreter tells the court I tried to rob him of ten shillings. Anne was a witness as were Mr Skillion and Mr Gray, so I got off that false charge. I went home and Ma tells me to tread carefully as the traps had it in for us Kelly's and our relly's. I always remembered what Ma told me that day and it was proven to be right all through me life.

CHAPTER FOUR

Now a partner

It was now eighteen seventy and I was over fifteen years old and bigger than most men. I was by now more like a partner to the notorious bushranger, Harry Power. One day we were riding through a neighbour's farm, Mr McBean's place it was to be sure, and there he was riding towards us and he calls out to Harry, 'Gooday Bill.' He must have thought Harry was Bill Frost. I could hardly believe it when Harry pulled out his revolver and said, 'I'll teach you to call me Bill, my name is Harry Power.'

I had not seen this side of Harry before and I did not like what I saw. Harry pointed his revolver at McBean's head and screamed at him to get off his horse. He then told him to tie his gold watch to the bridle, which the farmer did. Harry then took the horse and we headed off leaving the rich but sorry squatter to walk the three miles back to his home.

Harry taught me even more about bushcraft and shooting. I could now stalk a kangaroo and never miss a shot at even one hundred paces. I enjoyed our shooting contests that Harry organized about once a week. The big bushranger did not like to lose at anything, particularly at shooting. He would set up various sized targets at different distances and we took it in turns shooting at them. Harry would then get me to collect these targets, the last of which was usually only about the size of a ten bob note and about fifty paces away. Knowing Harry's temper and how he hated losing, I never hit this last target, until this one day when for some silly reason I plugged it right in the middle.

Harry then took his shot and he missed. In a violent rage he made me put up another target even smaller and further away. Then he fired at it and missed. Now I know I should have made sure I missed also, but as I was aiming me rifle Harry laughed and said something rude about me Ma and I flared up and quickly shot the target plumb in the centre. Well I thought Harry was going to throw a fit. He put his hand on the butt of his revolver, but I quickly said 'thank you Harry for teaching me to shoot nearly as good as you.' I could see that he was in two minds, then he smiled and told me that he did do a good job of teaching me.

We never did have any more shooting contests after that. Practise I did by meself after that, and I made the targets smaller and further away. Harry also showed me how to handle myself even better. He was very strong and taught me many holds and throws. As I grew bigger and stronger I was never beaten in the many fights I was often forced into.

It was in August of eighteen sixty nine that Ma's father James Quinn died. This upset Ma, so I stayed at home with her more now and looked after her. Whenever Ma was upset she would talk about her early days in Ireland. This seemed to help her so I would talk with her and ask her questions about those times. Ma at one time, when she was upset and talking freely, told me how a Thomas Quin, with just one N in his surname did visit sometimes, and occasionally stayed for a night or two.

Also Ma told me about my birth. She said I was a big baby, with hair the colour of copper. I was born at Ma's parents' home at Merri Creek and Ma told me that a neighbour, Mrs Gorman and Ma's mother did help at me birth. Father O'Hea baptized me a few days later in the Roman Catholic Church at Kilmore. Ma said they named me Edward after me dad's uncle and brother.

At the funeral of me grandfather, me wild uncles and relly's got drunk and started squabbling, so I stayed close to me Grannie. I offered to stay for a while to look after her but she said, 'I'm alright Neddie, your mother needs you.' I liked my Grannie and used to ask her to sing, but she just shakes her head and smiles. Then one day I asks her why she won't sing for me. Grannie cried and told me that she 'left all her singing behind in Ireland.'

It was not long after Ma's father's death that the bushranger Harry Power comes and takes me bush again to do what he calls business. I did not mind going 'bush' with Harry. He always made me cover me face whenever he did a stickup, or 'borrowed' some horses. A reward of two hundred pounds was placed on Harry's head. Many newspapers of the day reported that there was an unidentified youth helping "The notorious bushranger Harry Power".

One paper even said the description of this youth matched that of Edward Kelly. The end to me being partners with him came after we had been down Melbourne way and for some reason Harry does his temper and points his pistol at me and threatens to shoot me. I off home and tells me Ma, and to her joy I tells her I want nothing more to do with Harry.

I was to get a shock about a week later when Superintendent Nicolas with three other traps arrest me. Dan and all me family were watching while they took me away and they all heard the superintendent say, 'I'll take all of you in someday.' I was held for a month or so mainly at Benalla, and when they finally tried me I was discharged because there were no witnesses. When I got back home me Ma said she would shoot that Power if he showed his face around here again. I says, 'No you won't Ma, I will.' But that ended me notorious days with the wild bushranger who now had a price of two hundred pounds on his head. We did not have to worry about Harry anymore because the traps nabbed him while he was asleep in one of his hideouts.

Harry spread the word that I dobbed on him by telling the traps where he was, but it was one of the Lloyds who did, and in so doing got the now five hundred pounds reward which they shared around. Well Harry Power got fifteen years in Pentridge so I was lucky I left him when I did. Or was I?

CHAPTER FIVE

Lookout Neddie

The traps were closing in and hounded us all at every opportunity. They created false opportunities and one day they arrests Ma and charges her with selling liquor without a licence. Witnesses were called but each one in turn said they knew nothing of Mrs Kelly ever selling grog, so Ma was free to go, and she did, and she made a bit more grog.

Then they comes and grabs me and locks me up on a stealing charge, but I proved that I was nowhere near where the stealing took place. I knew who did that job but I would not tell the traps. I had to spend that Christmas in gaol and not long after getting home a Mr Isaiah Wright better known as Wild Wright, called at our place saying that he had lost his horse and could he please borrow one. I lends this Mr. Wright my horse and off he goes to town. Shortly after I spots his horse in our back paddock so I decides to take this very horse to town to swap back with my own. I tells Ma where I'm going and she says that she does not trust this Wild Wright and she says to me, 'Lookout Neddie.'

Like a fool I rides his horse, a big mare into town, mainly so I can get me own horse back. I am met in town by Constable Hall, who tells me to follow him. He leads me to the police station where he tells me to come in because he has some papers for me to sign. Now we all know that this Hall is a mean rough mongrel who has been known to have belted lots of young men so I am wary of this bully.

I refuse to get off me horse and Hall says, 'You're riding a stolen horse Ned Kelly. Now get off.' Before I can decide what to do the big constable, who stands about six and a half feet tall, grabs me by the collar and throws me to the ground.

This man who is supposed to uphold the law sees me bounce to me feet and shape up to him, so he pulls out his revolver and three times he tries to shoot me in cold blood. Luck is on me side so far as his gun would not fire. I was not going to wait for him to have any more tries to murder me, and I knew that if I turned to get away, and he could get his gun to work he would not hesitate to back shoot me so, what to do? I charges straight at him.

He is so surprised by someone not bowing down or being afraid of himself that I has no trouble knocking him down and throwing his revolver away. I wrestle him and get a good hold on him but he squeals like a stuck pig and calls for help. Sure me luck was out now, cause half a dozen nearby workers hears the big constable screaming and come and hold me. Then he belts me senseless with the butt of his revolver while they holds me.

Dr Hester from Wangaratta later puts nine stitches in me head. He told me he was going to report these injuries of mine to the Police at Wangaratta, but it did not seem to help me and I was then charged with receiving a stolen horse, found guilty, and sentenced to three years hard labour. At that trial I saw clearly how corrupt the system really was. Constable Hall told direct lies, saying I attacked him. I was given no chance. I would have, if allowed, called several witnesses to truthfully swear how this overgrown thug had bashed them in the past. No mention was made of how he had tried to shoot me, and I was only alive because his pistol did not fire.

Not only did he lie, he, as reported in the newspaper, paid several sovereigns to James Murdoch to perjure himself by backing his story. Constable Hall was transferred out of Greta and had a nervous breakdown. But this could not help me as I was falsely locked up. In me head I could hear Ma saying, 'Lookout Neddie, lookout Neddie, lookout Neddie.' Every three months I was allowed a visitor or a letter, but none of our family could get to Melbourne where I was locked up, so I looked forward to me occasional letter from home.

The earliest news I did get was from me Brother Jim who now twelve, had left school to look after the house. It was so good to get news from home, and Jim was a good writer. Jim writes that he did part time work for Mr Gould and Mr Krafft. This Mr Krafft one time camps near the eleven mile creek and asks Ma if he could put a few horses in her paddock. Ma tells him he can, and one morning me brothers Dan and Jim decides to take a couple of em for a ride. Mr Krafft goes into town and comes back with the new policeman in Greta, constable Flood. Flood a married man arrests me brothers and locks em up. Ma defends them in court and makes Krafft look silly and they get off.

This must have made the police more determined to "get" us Kelly's and our rellys, because it was not too long before Ma and Jane Graham were charged with stealing a saddle. In court Ma produced the receipt for the sale of the saddle, and the case was dismissed. Jim's letter goes on to tell me that Constable rotten Flood keeps coming back and flirts with me Sister Annie, and it's not long before she is pregnant. Ma, the letter tells me, fronts this Flood asking him what his intentions are. Well apparently his intentions were not good because he did not call again, not that he was seen to do at least. But Ma says he did come back when there was nobody at home, and he stole most of me horses. Ma fronts him again and he says to me Ma, 'Who is going to believe you against the word of a Policeman.' I keeps this letter and read it many times.

Me hatred towards traps was now higher than ever. Months later I gets another letter from home and I'm sad to read that me sister died giving birth to a daughter. This daughter Ma looks after, but the little one gets diphtheria and is soon to join her mother in the cemetery.

I by now am at boiling point with me anger, so I works harder and harder. Me sentence was hard labour, and it was hard. I worked in the rock quarries at Point Gellibrand, where it got very hot, and the warders were strict but consistent, so after watching them for a while I could usually work out their ways and how they wanted things to work on their shift.

I don't know how I would have got through those hard times if it was not for Father O'Hea. He visited me regular and took me confessions. Sometimes he brought me news from home. We would pray in me tiny cell, and I remember him the first time he came in, he said with a grin a mile wide, 'Well Ned it is lucky you haven't a cat cause there is no room to swing it.' Yes Father O'Hea was indeed me saviour, and little did I know it but he would be there again one day when I needed him.

I, along with about one hundred and twenty other chosen, well behaved prisoners, was transferred to Port Phillip Bay, to live in a ship stationed there as a prison ship because Pentridge was overcrowded. It was much better there, and the food was good. I was given a clay pipe and a daily ration of tobacco as well. For this we were expected to work hard building seawalls from the rocks cut from the quarries. Stonemasonry they called it, and I did well, and liked the hard skilful work.

It was in February eighteen seventy four that I was escorted to the front gate of Pentridge Prison to sign me release papers. I thinks that I really do not want to come back here especially when the releasing officer laughs as he says 'See you soon Ned Kelly.' I glares back at him but did not give him the pleasure of a comment back to him. Most of the warders had been good to me in me three wasted years, so I held no grudges to them, as they had their job to do.

Me clothes that I wore in were the ones I had to wear out, and they were about three sizes too small, as I had grown so much. The new train service was in, and it takes me all the way to Glenrowan. I then has only a few miles to walk home. Nervous I was, to be sure, as I hurried along the track to Greta. Would anyone be home I wondered, and would they know me, after all I had grown so much. This was going to be the first time I will have seen me family for years.

But me butterflies disappears soon as I sees the person who did bring me into this world. Ma met me in the yard as she had seen me walking up the track. 'Neddie, my how you've grown my son.' I stood and looked at me Ma, then I told her how much I had missed her and all me brothers and sisters.

By now me kinfolk were lined up in order to greet me. Maggie was now sixteen with a baby in her arms was first in line. She married a no hoper named Skillion, I hold Maggie, then gives a kiss to her and her baby. Then I looks for little Dan, but there was a young wiry, tough looking critter next in line. 'Where is Dan Kelly?' I says with me best grin. 'Right here Ned Kelly,' comes this man's voice back at me, and with that he attempts to throw me to the ground like he used to do years ago. Kate tells us to stop it and rushes to greet me. 'Welcome home Ned,' she blurts out amongst her tears. I then turns to me little sister Grace who is now nearly nine. 'I remember you,' she yells to me as she runs to me. And I have not time to say a word to her before she was in me arms saying, 'You used to sing to me, and you are my biggest brother in the world and will you sing to me again, cause I missed you too much.' To be sure, I am where I truly wants to be, "Home."

We go inside and talk for ages. I learned from Dan that he was already a trap hater and that he was sick of them always hounding our family. I already knew but Ma tells me that Jim is in gaol. Then Ma takes me aside and tells me the full story of how Annie was seduced by that mongrel Flood, and how she died a horrible death giving birth to her child who did not live much more than a year. After a while I goes out to check on me beloved horses but most of em were gone. 'It were Flood that took em,' Ma said. I then tells me Ma that one day I would settle with this Flood. Ma says that he had been transferred to Oxley, and he is reported to be scared to death that you are going to "get" him.

Later on that night after eating me homecoming meal of roast lamb, peas, roast praties, or potatoes as we now calls em, we all had a sing along round the kitchen fire. Ma is in fine voice as she leads us in many songs, mainly Irish Folk ones she remembers from her childhood in Ireland. Dan and I stops singing and listen in awe as the Kelly girls sing in perfect harmony "Sweet Molly Malone," and several other beautiful songs, some that they had made up also. Three years of stored up tension seemed to flow out me eyes in the form of tears when me little nine year old sister sings solo for a start, then is joined by me other Sisters Maggie and Kate, in their rendition of "Silent Night." Ma then makes the evening complete by cooking some pancakes smothered in honey, which we washes down with hot cocoa.

The next morning I wakes up early and quietly goes outside, thinking I would be the first to wake, but there was me brother Dan dressed in oversized clothes, grooming his horse. 'Morning Dan,' I say. Dan looks at me and I can sense he is not too sure about things. I work out that this is most likely cause I have been away for so long and he has gotten used to being the man of the house.

'Mornin,' shouts me brother, 'it's nearly the middle of the bleedin day.' I walks over and strokes his horse's muzzle and tells him I am proud of him for being the man about the place, and if he was happy about it I would like to share the workload. Dan nods to me and says, 'I missed you Ned, don't go away again.' We both are quiet for a moment, then Dan grins and says, 'I bet I can outride you.' We saddle up and ride, then ride some more, till finally I nods to Dan and tells him that he sure can ride. This seems to do the trick and Dan is now smiling, and I can feel that we are Kelly Brothers again.

After breakfast Ma tells me that she was in love with a wonderful man named George King and she would be pleased if I would stand alongside em when they married. 'I was waiting till you came home Neddie.' So two weeks later I did stand as witness as me Ma married this twenty three year old American. As witness I has to sign the wedding certificate, which I does and I sees that Ma, who cannot read or write, had signed with an x. Then I sees that her new husband, who is a very good writer has also signed with an x. He must have done this so Ma won't feel too bad about being illiterate.

I grows to like George and found that he soon become one of us. He liked horses and had spent a little time inside for horse stealing, and he was a natural fighter, not really a boxer as such but a rough and tumble fighter, and he taught me some good body punches which would prove to help me before much longer. I worked hard and set up a makeshift punching bag out the back of our house which I tore into most mornings and evenings.

CHAPTER SIX

A score is settled

My main idea after being released from that hellhole called Pentridge was to find honest work, and me first job was at Moya about six mile away. I worked hard from sunup till sunset, felling stringy barks and red gums. We then had to tow this timber by bullock teams to the mill. Bullock Teams are big strong, well trained steers hitched together with a long chain joined up to all their harnesses, which trails behind them and we joins this chain to the log. The driver, or handler, walks alongside these fine animals and talks to them as he cracks a big whip.

I was probably in me prime and still felt me hatred to this, Wild Wright, for who I had to be locked away for years. I didn't go looking for him because I didn't want any trouble, especially as I did not want to give the traps any reason to lock me away. I mostly worked seven days each week, but one weekend the boss said that we were not going to work, so I rides to Beechworth that Saturday afternoon to have a quiet drink.

I goes into the Imperial hotel and had not even finished me first drink when I hears this voice that I could never forget, not after serving time for his crime. Anyway he must have seen me come in cause to make himself appear bigger in front of the group of rough looking men he was drinking with, he looks over at me and says in a deliberately vicious tone, 'Men first, dogs come last.'

Of course this brought jeers and loud laughter from his group. But you could have heard a pin drop when I gets up and walks over to stand in front of him with me fists clenched.

'Well if it's not young Ned,' he spits out. 'Steal any good horses lately.' Three years of hatred towards this man came to a boiling point right there and then, and I started towards him, but the big publican jumps in and says, 'Not in here.' So with all and sundry following, he leads us out the back where he supplied us with boxing uniforms, and tells us we must fight by the Marquis of Queensberry rules of boxing.

He then tells us the winner will be recognised as the bare-knuckle boxing champion of North East Victoria. He then told us the rules that we had to abide by to become this champion. Then he draws a line in the dirt and tells us to stand either side of it. I am still worked up and I nearly starts swinging even while the Publican, who is the referee, is talking, but luckily I don't. Settling down a bit I listens to his rules. 'Whatever happens' he says, 'you must come back to this line,' He tells us the end of a round is not timed, but is determined when blood is drawn, or there is a knockdown.

Each man has a picker up and has thirty seconds to get his boxer back into a fit enough state to get to the line ready to fight, which he must do within eight seconds of reaching the line. I was probably better off with this delay as I had cooled a little, and I gathered me wits, realizing that I was facing up to the toughest, meanest, most vicious fighter in all of Victoria.

Me body became ready, and just as it did when years ago I saved young Dick Shelton from drowning. Me head cleared and a calmness came over me. I glared towards Wild Wright and held eye contact with him and I felt a surge of confidence when he broke eye contact first.

Here I was nineteen years old, six foot tall, twelve stone heavy, and there he was, an inch taller and a stone or so heavier, but I reckoned that he had more fat on him than I did. All me hard work had made me fit and strong. He must have looked like a winner as he jumped around sparring at mid-air, but I never took me eyes off his. By now about half the town of Beechworth must have gathered around us and a big group of Wild Wright's mates were now yelling for him to kill me. The publican called us to the line and told us to fight, which we surely did that day. I sensed he was trying the old trick of smashing me nose in, so I used me speed and footwork. Each time he tried a haymaker at me nose I parried the blow with me left and hit him a couple of hard body blows, which shook him up. I was feeling good and continued to box and hit him in the ribs under his heart. Even when he hit me I truly did not suffer and I found that I could hit him almost at will. Blood was drawn by both, and the rounds began to mount up.

After fifteen rounds I knew I had the better of this mongrel that I had served those years in gaol for. I, for the next five rounds fought him in the only way I could. I beat him senseless, and after twenty rounds the man recognized as unbeatable could not fight on.

The referee announced that I was the official bare knuckle boxing champion of North East Victoria. This I did not really care about, instead I was happy to have given him his just deserts. After this, I noticed people everywhere looked at me in a different way. Me Brother Dan was pleased when I got home and I told him all about the fight. 'You're a legend Ned,' he tells me. Wherever I went after the fight, I would hear people talk about me.

One day as I was riding down the road in Greta I heard a youngster yell, 'Look its Ned Kelly.'

About a dozen more youngsters come running and stood around me. 'Please Mr Kelly, tell us how you beat that nasty Wild Wright man.' I gets off me horse and sits on the ground with them and tells em all about how I was wrongfully put in gaol because Wild Wright would not tell the truth, but set me up to do his sentence. I went on telling them about the fight, and answering their questions for about an hour, then as I was riding away I heard one em shout.

'I WANT TO BE AS GAME AS NED KELLY.'

Another lad yelled back, 'NOBODY IS AS GAME AS NED KELLY.' I ride away back home and on the wayback I can't stop smiling and I starts singing, "Oh Danny Boy."

My singing seemed to attract firstly one, then gradually more Willy wagtail birds, and soon I was crooning me favourite song with the backing of about a dozen whistling little black and white friends. These wagtails have always been a favourite of me Ma, and she can often be heard whistling back to them and calling out, 'good morning Mrs Pretty.' My little friends accompanied me to nearly back home, but they suddenly disappeared and I knew that something was astray, so I stopped singing and approached our place more carefully. Sure enough the little birds were a sure sign of warning to me.

I draws me pistol and approached to where four men on horseback were about to open the gate to the stockyards of me horses. 'Stop now and don't move or I will shoot,' I yelled. They did not stop but galloped off, so I shot the hat off the leading rider who I knew to be the head stockman of Mr Whitty, the rich farmer who had been known to have stolen horses and cattle and sold them on. 'Tell

Whitty that Ned Kelly will not just shoot a hat next time,' I yelled after the four scared rustlers. Dan came at the run and after seeing what happened apologised for not keeping a better eye out on the place. Dan drew his pistol and fired a shot at the now out of range riders.' We'll have to pay this Whitty another visit,' I tells me brother.

I grew closer to my stepfather George King and we started a business of buying or "finding" cattle and horses and selling them for a profit. Me Ma told me and George many times to be careful as the traps were on the lookout for us. This work was easier than what I had been doing since my release from gaol. I had done many jobs and had had no trouble finding work. One time I was doing some fencing at Mr Bailey's vineyard, and when I had finished Mr Bailey asks me to do some repairs to his stone cellar. A local selector and builder Mr Heinreich Freitag was visiting the Baileys and noticed my stonework and employed me to build the stone walls for his house on his property called "Fernley," at Chesney Veale near the swamp at Winton. I got me Brother Dan and a couple of friends to help me. I was proud of that job, and Mr Freytag gave me a bonus. I did carve the year eighteen seventy five above the back door and I remember me little brother wanted to carve his name alongside it but I would not let him.

While we were away working, Ma gives birth to a boy, whom they named John. Young John, me half Brother could not wait to come into this world and comes in March, and it is a traveller that brings Dan and me the news. We knocks off work early that day and has a drink to celebrate.

We finished that job at Christmas eighteen seventy five.

We got back to Ma's to celebrate me twenty first birthday, and I gets to meet and hold me new little half Brother. Dan lines up for a hold of this "Little John" as Dan names him, and that's what our new half Brother was called by Dan from then on. 'Look at the little blighter,' me brother says, 'you can see he's going to be a natural horseman just like me, Dan Kelly.' "Little John" and Dan were inseparable after that, and I reckons it won't be too long before Dan has the boy on a horse. Then as it is me birthday, Ma gives a little speech and she near brought tears to me eyes when she thanked her Neddie for looking out for her and all the families. Being twenty one years old did not really mean as much to me as it probably did to other young men, as I had been doing a man's work, and have had to take on a man's responsibility, for several years now.

But it was a nice party with no fights, which is a rare thing with some of the wild rellys that were there. A couple of times I did have to glare at some of the menfolk and they seemed to get the message that I would not put up with any nonsense at this party that Ma had given me. Yes, I worked hard then, and in eighteen seventy six I got me job back at Sounders and Rule sawmills on the bank of the Burkes Hole Creek north of Greta. We cut the sleepers for the railway between Wangaratta and Beechworth. I must have been a pretty good worker, cause here, like most of the other places I worked, I was made a leading hand and got more pay than the other workers.

It was in that year the traps tried to pin a horse stealing charge on me. Henri Lydeker was missing a horse and reckoned I must have stolen it. The traps jumped at this chance and I was charged but defended meself and won the case. At the time Tom Lloyd and I were helping Ma's brother John to round up his stock on Leydeker's property.

There was some disagreement between me Uncle John and Leydeker over the cost of me uncle having leased his horses on Leydeker's property, so me uncle gave him a good horse as payment. This very horse went missing and Leydeker reported it to the Police, who as usual were very eager to pin a charge on me or me rellys. It were a chap by the name of Woodyard that was eventually charged.

Then the traps charged Dan with stealing a saddle which he had paid for. When his trial came I defended him and produced a receipt for the saddle and the case was thrown out of court. It was becoming clear to me that the Police were willing and in fact keen to pin any charge on us Kelly's, so I thinks that I better tread even more carefully.

I had to use me fist a bit those days, and one time I fronted this Mr Whitty who had spread the word that I, Ned Kelly had stolen his prize bull. Whitty changed his mind and I did not hurt him too much. I did not steal his bull. It was well known that Whitty was generous towards the traps, and it was quite common to see a trap riding a good horse when everyone knew he could not afford to buy such a good expensive animal.

I found it was much easier work trading in horses and cattle. We had a camp at Bullock Creek. Dan and a couple of his mates Joe Byrne and Aaron Sherritt joined us in our business there. Our business grew and before long young Tom Lloyd, who later was to play an important part in our lives, joins Wild Right, Bill Williamson, Mick Woodyard, and Allen Loury in our "business."

Wild Wright was now accepted into the family and respectfully called me Ned and did as I said. We became known as the "Greta Mob" and had many sympathisers, but not from the rich squatters who had the traps in their pockets.

The traps shut their eyes to Whitty and other squatters impounding any animals they found wandering and then sold them. Now I ask of anyone, what was the difference between what we were doing and what these squatters were doing? The final straw came when Whitty put in the local newspaper that they would impound all cattle and other animals that they found and sue the owners for trespassing. Another well to do squatter, a Mr. Andrew Byrne joins in with Whitty and it seemed as though they claimed all the territory as theirs.

The traps backed them of course, with some money changing hands. In one day Whitty and his cronies impounded over sixty head belonging to the poor farmers. Finally this rich squatter made a big mistake and impounded two mares with fillies at foot, belonging to me and Tom Lloyd.

Well I had had enough, so Tom and me breaks the locks to his pound and we takes back our horses. Whitty spread the word that we stole his horses, which we had not.

It was about this time that me Brother Dan and his friend Steve Hart was arrested, charged and found guilty of horse stealing. Dan was sent to Beechworth Gaol for twelve months. They did not take those horses, as we told the traps. By now all of us "Greta Mob" had reached boiling point, so we reckoned we'd pay this arrogant Whitty a visit. So in August eighteen seventy seven, I with my good friend Joe Byrne, on a bright moonlit night went to Whitty's new station at Myrrhee and helped ourselves to eleven of his best horses. They were worth about a hundred and seventy pound between them. We drove them to Boorgunyah on the Murray River and crossed over it into New South Wales. We changed their brands, sold them and returned home.

CHAPTER SEVEN

I meets Fitzpatrick

I am now twenty two years of age and I am recognized as the leader of our "mob" so I travels around a lot. One time when I was in the Commercial Hotel in Benalla, I met a young constable by chance. He was talking rough and with some people I know so I thought maybe he wasn't too bad. I prove meself wrong this time. He came over and offered me a drink so I took it and we talked. He told me he had just completed his police training and had not long been in Benalla and had not known much about the area. 'Do you know me?' I asks him. 'No,' he replied, 'but you seem okay.'

He told me his name was Fitzpatrick, Alexander Fitzpatrick. 'I am Ned Kelly' I tells him.

'Yes now I know you,' he said, 'but as I said you don't seem so bad. I laughed and he poured more drink into me mug. I didn't usually drink much, in fact I had never been drunk before, so I left after a few drinks. As I got outside I felt funny as though I might be drunk. I got to me horse and out comes Fitzpatrick and the mongrel arrests me for being drunk.

I later went back to the hotel and asks the publican what was going on. 'I am sorry Ned but the trap told me to put something which he gave me into your drink.'

I was furious and when I next sees Fitzpatrick he was alone so I walked up to him and told him what I thought of him and he said he was now a copper which had arrested, 'The Ned Kelly,' and he laughed.

So what did I do, I did what I must do. I knocks him unconscious. When he comes round I told him that next time I'll "fix" him much worse. He gets up and said he would not charge me and he is sorry about it all but he wanted to get his job off to a good start. 'Remember what I said,' I tells him. After that we spoke each time we crosses paths, and I thought the bad times were over with this Fitzpatrick, but I was so wrong.

I had sort of befriended Fitzpatrick and he sometimes called in at our house. He said he was an Irish man and he showed no more signs of hounding us until Dan and his cousins Tom and John Lloyd got into trouble pinching some groceries. We got word that a warrant had been issued for Dan and Tom's arrest for stealing, so the two of them took to the bush. Fitzpatrick came and told me that if I brought them in he would get the charges dropped. I foolishly believed this conman, this liar, and I probably, now filled with hope of getting me brother and his friend off free, goes and talk's em into coming with me to this Fitzpatrick.

The cocky young Policeman smiled, and said all would be alright. Well at their hearing the charges were not dropped, and they each were sentenced to three months hard labour. I immediately invites Fitzpatrick outside to settle this, but the coward hides in the police station. I thinks to meself, 'Ned you have a lot to learn.' And there is the easy way and the hard way to learn, so what does I do? I takes the hard way.

Over the next few weeks I became attached to a pretty young lass and spent many nights away from home. Ma tells me that it was about time I found a nice girl and settled down, but I did not answer her comments, but I was quite keen on this girl who has already mentioned that scary Marriage word to me. But I am not for thinking too much about such a big move, though I am not too sure what she has in mind.

Then it was time for me brother's release. Dan had changed a bit while being in the hellhole, and on Ma's advice, two days after his release, I takes him and me best mate Joe Byrne away for the sheep shearing season. I had hoped this work would help keep me brother out of trouble, and it did for a while. It was good hard work sheep shearing, and we were making good honest money. Dan grew to like this work, and said to me after a few weeks up in the Riverland's that he reckoned he'd had enough of gaol and wanted to stop horse stealing and misbehaving and wanted to go straight, and maybe settle down.

I looks at me now not so little brother and says 'Alright then. We'll do that Dan. What about you going straight as well?' I asks Joe Byrne. 'I probably could not lie straight in bed,' replies he. We all laugh and are feeling good, and I thinks it is good for all of us to work hard and to keep out of trouble. Then Joe breaks the mood by saying that he thought we had no hope. 'We're bloody Irish and the traps will get us no matter,' he says. Dan shakes his head and says that he's never going back to that rotten gaol.

We were surprised a few days later when me stepfather George King turns up. 'You're Ma is due to have a baby soon,' he tells us. I am surprised that he did not stay with Ma and I asks him why he wasn't with her in her hour of need. George shrugs his shoulders and does not answer.

Later he tells us that the word is out that the traps are onto us and are going to trump up a charge of us stealing Whitty's horses. A couple more weeks of hard work go by and I worries about Ma and I asks me stepfather if he is going back to be with her while their baby is born. He does not answer me so I grabs him and gives him a good shake and tell him to answer me. He tells me he's not going back and that's that. I decides that I'm going home and Dan and Joe agree to come.

We are just about to head off back to Greta when George King says that Constable Fitzpatrick has been hanging around our sister Kate and Ma is worried. When we got home Ma had already given birth to a baby girl. I breaks the news about George not coming back to her. She says she half expected as much because he reckoned Fitzpatrick was up to no good and would one day get us all locked up. I picks up Ma's new born baby, me stepsister, and for some reason I says, 'Hello little Alice. You will be a fine daughter and a great help to your mother.'

Ma tells us that Fitzpatrick had been and said he had a warrant for Dan's arrest. I asks Ma about Fitzpatrick and me Sister Kate and Ma's expression changes straight away, and she tells me that he had been making advances to Kate. A few days after we got back home Joe Byrne and I were tending to some of our horses when the mongrel turns up with his trumped up reason to arrest Dan. Me brother was eating his meal and he asks Fitzpatrick if he could finish it. 'Take your time, I'll wait while you get changed also,' says the trap. Meanwhile Joe and I are on our way back to the house when we hears me sister screaming, so I runs inside just in time to see Fitzpatrick point his pistol at me Ma.

He pulls the trigger before I can do anything, but he had not allowed for Dan who as quick as lightning is onto him and wrestles the swine to the floor just as his pistol goes off and the ceiling collects the lead that Fitzpatrick meant to murder Ma with. Dan wrestles the gun off him and I pulls out me own pistol and tells Dan to back away because I was going to shoot this mongrel.

Dan throws Fitzpatrick hard against the wall and the trap falls and cuts his wrist on the door handle. I aim me gun at him and call him a coward, and this vermin who was by now crying like a newborn baby says, 'Don't hurt me Ned. I won't say anything of what happened. Please let me go.' I asks Ma what has happened and she tells me that Fitzpatrick had dragged Kate onto his knee and was making advances on her, so says Ma, 'I hit him on his head with the fire shovel.' Joe Ryan and William Skillion who had been eating a meal, both piped up and supported Ma's description of the events.

Well I then tells Fitzpatrick that I should shoot him like the dog that he is, he again begs me to let him go and he promises to say nothing of this. I gets Ma to bandage his wrist and I now can see the mongrel is quite drunk. 'I won't even mention I was here. We Irish have got to stick together,' he says and stretches his hand out to shake mine. I do not shake his hand and I tells him he is not an Irishman's bootlace and that he was an Englishman that was born here.

I yells at him, 'you are nothing but a lying coward.' Then I opens the door and tells him to go and to pray that we never meet again. Fitzpatrick staggers out the door then quietly tells me to take Dan away cause they have a warrant out for us. I asks him if me Ma was in any trouble and he gave me his word that he would not say anything to anyone about what happened here tonight. The drunken coward manages to mount his horse and leaves.

Well I thinks, maybe we should get away until things settle down, so we have a bit of a family talk and Dan and I decides to go bush for a while. Joe Byrne says he's for coming and says Steve Hart will want to come also. I have an uneasy feeling inside me, but there is not really a choice for us.

CHAPTER EIGHT

We are the Kelly Gang

Joe Byrne gallops off to pack his gear and to get Steve Hart. Dan and I pack our guns and plenty of ammunition as well as two pack horses laden with supplies. Then it's time to say goodbye to Ma, but it's not easy to leave her. 'Neddie,' she says you must promise to look out for Dan.' I tells her I will and I watch as she says her goodbyes to Dan, then she pushes him towards me and says to me 'look after him, he were a lot of trouble getting born so don't let him go to waste, you hear me Neddie.' I kisses me Ma and again gives me promise to look after me brother. 'Go' she yells, 'my soul with you.'

We headed to our hideout at Bullock Creek and it was not long before we were joined by Joe and Steve. I tells em all the facts, which are that Dan and I are now on the run until at least things settle down. I tells Joe and Steve that they do not have to join us, but if they do they will be hunted as well. Joe Byrne me mate since childhood, tells me he's "in" and ready. Steve Hart, Dan's best friend says that he will be with us also.

We know we are pretty safe here at Bullock Creek as we have been doing our horse and cattle business from here for a long time now and had made our camp almost impossible to find. The next few days were quiet, then we were paid a visit by me Uncle Patrick Quinn and Wild Wright. They had brought us supplies and bad news.

They tells us that the morning after we left Greta and Ma, the traps comes and arrests Ma and charges her with aiding and abetting Edward Kelly in an attempt to murder constable Alexander Fitzpatrick. They tells us that the traps put Ma into a cart and took her and her new baby off to gaol and the word is that they will lock her up for a long time.

'Fitzpatrick,' I screams. 'Oh I should have shot that dirty lying swine.' I asks me uncle which gaol Ma was in. Me first thoughts were to break her and baby Alice out of one of the local gaols, but me uncle tells me the traps took them straight to Melbourne.

I thinks for a moment, then asks Patrick and Wild to go and see Magistrate Alfred Wyatt, who was thought of as a fair man. Me message to him was that Dan and I would give ourselves up in return for our mothers release and pardon. 'This must be put in writing,' I tells em as they head off.

We waited hopefully for a few days but the answer came back as no deal. We had in the past looked for and found a little gold here at Bullock Creek and me plan was to now raise as much money as we could to make an appeal after Ma's sentencing. To make more money we planted crops of barley to make moonshine, or illegal grog and sell it on. We did find more gold and Joe Byrne made several trips to some Chinese buyers.

We knew the traps would one day come looking for us so we built a fort with walls a couple of feet thick, and left slits for shooting through. Then we cleared the trees and scrub away for about a hundred yards all around our fort. We practiced shooting at targets placed at different distances around, and even Dan became quite a good shot. The lead we shot we would collect and melt down to remake our bullets.

Joe came back from selling gold with terrible news. The rotten system had combined to ignore the defence evidence given at Ma's trial, and Judge Barry had directed the jury, which consisted of at least one former trap, to find Ma guilty. Both Williamson and Skillion gave evidence that they saw Fitzpatrick make advances to Kate Kelly, and Mrs King, after warning him to stop, and when he did not, she gave him a light tap on his helmet to protect her daughter. They went on to describe how Dan, then I, wrestled him to the floor and he cut his wrist on the door in the scuffle. They also told the court how Fitzpatrick had tried to murder Mrs King but his bullet hit the ceiling in the scuffle.

Joe tells us that he was told that Kelly sympathisers in the crowd had spread the word that I was there and was going to shoot Fitzpatrick. The coward was seen to be openly crying and shaking during the trial. The traps must have believed I was there and Ma was heavily guarded the whole time.

THE SPIRIT OF NED

Joe goes on and says that this Judge Barry in sentencing Ma, tells her that if "Ned Kelly" was in the dock he would have given him twenty one years. The so called jury did as they were told and found me Ma guilty and Judge Barry is in his glory in sentencing me Ma, an innocent woman, to three years with labour. Then he announces that Skillion and Williamson were accomplices and gives them six years gaol with hard labour. I takes this news real hard and I grabs me guns and mount up only to see Dan doing the same. 'No Dan,' I says 'let me handle this.' 'She's my Ma too' he yells and mounts up. With revenge on our minds Dan and I ride for Greta and Fitzpatrick.

After riding our mounts too hard for the first mile or so I tells me brother to slow down and take it easy on the horses. 'Someone's following us' says Dan so we turn into the scrub and ready ourselves to ambush em. 'Bail up' I yells at the two galloping horsemen. Then I sees its Joe and Steve, so I asks em where they are going. 'Same place as you Ned' they say together. I looks at em and tell em that there will be big trouble and they don't have to be in it. 'We know what we are doing,' they say. Joe Byrne says it's too late anyway and that they part of the "Kelly Gang."

So, just before sundown the "Kelly Gang" with loaded guns rides down the main track to Greta ready to repay that Constable Fitzpatrick with more than just words. But we are met about a hundred yards before the police station by a group of a dozen or more armed riders. Tom Lloyd was at the front and says 'don't do it Ned.'

I says 'either join us or step aside Tom.' He tells me that it would do no good shooting up the police station cause the traps have transferred Fitzpatrick miles away, and he is now a drunken nervous wreck. 'Go back to your hideout Ned, you can do more good for your mother from there.' I tells Tom we will take his advice, but if that mongrel Fitzpatrick was here I would have shot him. We do take the advice of our good friend Tom Lloyd and ride back to Bullock Creek, taking with us more ammunition given to us by Tom and the Greta mob. Once we had looked after our horses and had a feed, I calls a meeting. I tells all of the three men here with me that I am grateful for the support they had just shown, and that I was proud of them. We discussed our position and our next plan of action. I insisted that each of them spoke their mind and they did. It was a good meeting, and afterwards we all shook hands and swore allegiance to each other and the "Kelly Gang."

Tom Lloyd had also passed on some newspapers, and one front page story featured the report from the police magistrate at Benalla which stated that he was, "appalled at the treatment and sentence given out to Mrs King." He stated, "that in forty years of working in the legal field he had never seen anything like it."

With the help of me good friend Joe Byrne, I writes many letters trying to get freedom for me Ma. We raise as much money as we can for an appeal for her. While waiting for Ma's appeal I practises me shooting a lot and I imagines the targets I was aiming at were really Fitzpatrick and Judge Barry, and I hardly missed me shots. I do remember missing a target one day when all four of us "Kelly Gang" Were practising, and as I missed me Brother Dan says 'imagine Flood is standing there Ned.' I does and hit the target dead centre.

It is now October eighteen seventy eight, and as he has done on many occasions, Tom Lloyd pays us a welcome visit. Tom tells me that a trap by the name of Strahan had been to see me Uncle Patrick and had promised to pay him one hundred pounds if he would lead the traps to our hideout. 'Did me uncle take the money,' I asks. Tom says that Patrick told Strahan that he would, if they promised not to shoot us, and Strahan the mongrel tells him that he 'would shoot Ned Kelly down like a dog.' Tom Lloyd says that Patrick would then not show em where the gang was hiding.

'Tell me uncle that Ned Kelly said that Patrick Quinn will be a dead man if he helps those traps.' Not long after Tom Lloyd's visit, me Sister Maggie, an excellent rider comes with supplies and more news. News that we were expecting, which meant no more shooting practise. 'The traps are somehow sure that the Kelly Gang is hiding out in the Wombat Ranges,' Maggie tells us. I quickly asks if Uncle Patrick did "dob" us in, and Maggie said she was not sure but rumour has it that four traps will head off from Mansfield, and another four will head off the other end. 'They are both leaving on Friday, and Tom Lloyd said to watch out as they have at least one of the latest Spencer Repeating Rifles which can fire twenty shots a minute.'

Maggie cries as she says, 'Ned be careful, they are bragging that they are going to shoot you on sight.' I thanks me sister and tells her not to worry cause those traps could not hit the side of a barn with a handful of wheat.

Then she tells me she was talking to Dr Nicholson and he said that the little scratches on Fitzpatrick's wrist could not have been caused by a bullet and that the officer was drunk when he attended to him. She is still upset as she says, 'they have put a price of one hundred pounds on your head Ned.' Again I tells Maggie not to worry. Before Maggie leaves I gives her a letter to give to the newspaper to print.

I writes that I feel more keenly than I can express, the unjust treatment handed out to me mother, who was arrested with a baby at her breast and convicted of a crime of which she was innocent.

THE SPIRIT OF NED

After me sister left I calls the boys together and explains about the two parties of traps coming to bounty hunt us. I tells em that we will scout around and keep an eye on where they are and we will work out our plan of action. I remind Dan, Steve, and Joe that we must tread carefully as the traps are planning to shoot us on sight and share the money for doing so. Joe Byrne stands up and says 'so it's alright for them swines to try to murder your mother falsely, put a price on our heads, then come and murder us to get pay for it?'

That night we gathered round the fire inside our fort, as we did most nights and talked, and sometimes one or all of would sing, usually it were Irish songs or poems we liked most. This night as we all drank a mug of coffee, things were quieter than usual, especially Joe Byrne who were sullen and moody, and sat away from us a bit. He did not join in as Dan picked up his bush "Banjataer" as he called it. Dan, me clever little brother had made this musical instrument out of bush timber and the strings were of the bark from a stringybark tree. He had tightened these ten strings at different tensions so some sounded like guitar and some like banjo. Dan played his "Banjataer" and then Joe speaks his first words for hours, he says, 'don't play that thing Daniel.' Me brother strums a bit louder then says to Joe 'Me names Dan, Dan Kelly, and I'll ask you to not call me Daniel ever again Joe Byrne.'

I ready meself to step between them as Joe gets up and walks over to Dan who has quietly put down his "Banjataer." Joe stops in front of the now standing Dan and both are looking each other squarely in the eye, neither ready to back down. 'I've watched you grow from a little lad into a man Dan Kelly, now sit you down and strum me a melody and I'll be tellin you a poem I has writ just for you.' I grins as Dan strums away as Joe Byrne stands, bows to us then recites his poem,

'Dan Kelly, who is he you said?

He is the lad who lived in the shadow of Ned.

He is the one who can ride as good as any man.

Don't call him Daniel, he prefers Dan.

Dan, Dan Kelly,

He has fire in his belly.

He has had it rough,

But this man is tough.

Persecuted, forced to go on the run.

Forced to be a man he missed youth's fun.

> *He left school before the bell was rung.*
> *Chased by the traps, now part of the Kelly gang.*
> *True to his kin and mother,*
> *He's a man, just like his brother.*
> *And if there's a fight in the air,*
> *I'm on the side of this Kelly pair.*
> *Live on Dan Kelly when we have died.*
> *'Look out for Dan his mother cried.'*
> *So live on Dan Kelly when we have all gone.*
> *Your mother said you were special the day you were born.*
> *And I say you're special this very day,*
> *So play your music and hear what I say.*
> *Live on Dan Kelly, that's what I said*
> *Live on Dan Kelly, proud brother of Ned.'*

Me brother gets up and thanks Joe Byrne for his poem, and they shake hands. Not one to be left out of anything Dan's best mate Steve Hart jumps up and beckoning me to join him he starts singing,

> *'Oh Danny boy,*
> *The pipes the pipes are calling,*
> *From glen to glen and down the mountain side,.'*

So all is well and we sing and talk for hours, then I says that from tomorrow on we must be quiet and have no fires, 'cause the traps are due and I wants us to surprise them, not them surprise us.'

CHAPTER NINE

They come to Stringybark

I wakes early the next morning only to find Joe Byrne is already up and has made a billy of tea over a small well screened fire. I thanks him for doing the right thing towards me brother last night. He shrugs his shoulders and tells me he meant every word of his poem, and that if things got nasty then he would help me get Dan away somehow. 'You know' me best mate says to me in his solemn voice, which is when he is thinking deeply, 'Dan was telling me that he learnt a bit about South Africa at school and he reckons the English are victimising the Afrikaans and Natives there, like they are here to us. He told me that he would love to go there and help the locals in some way.' I nods and tells me mate that I knew this and that maybe things might work out for Dan. Joe and I ate a little cold damper with honey washed down with tea, then after telling Dan and Steve where we were going we headed off to spy on the oncoming traps.

It wasn't till mid-afternoon that we spotted four traps a few miles from our hideout at Bullock Creek. They were each leading a pack horse with body straps hanging off the back of them. From the cover of thick scrub and trees we had no trouble seeing that they had a Spencer repeating rifle as well as a shotgun and other rifles and revolvers. We watched as they rode slightly away from our hideout, then we headed back to our camp, and Joe was fuming mad. He started kicking things and yelling madly. Steve Hart asks Joe Byrne what is wrong. 'Traps dressed as prospectors, plain clothed bounty hunters, that's what's wrong.'

I takes over and explain that four traps are not far from here, so as soon as they make camp I have a plan to surround them, bail em up and take their weapons, especially the new spencer rifle. Joe stills goes on, and tells Dan and Steve about the body straps the traps have on their pack horses ready to cart our bodies away. 'Murder us, that's what they plan,' he screams. I tells Joe not to worry because the traps won't be finding us, we will be surprising them.

Just on dusk we hears a shotgun blast about a mile away, so I takes Dan and we go for a look. We head towards the area I reckoned the shot came from, and not long after I sees a lone trap heading towards the old shingle hut which is only a mile from our camp. I tell Dan that it looks like Constable Strahan, the trap who had been bragging he was going to shoot me. We follow him and he goes into the shingle hut where it must be their camp for at least tonight. We move closer and can see that there are four traps inside, and it looks to me that the mongrel Flood is one of them. Dan and I have seen enough and we go back to where Joe and Steve are waiting for us.

I go through me plan for tomorrow, then we check our weapons to make sure they are ready. Sleep does not come easily that night. I pray a lot, mainly for the safety of me brother, and prays that the traps will bail up when I tells em to. The main mission is to disarm em and take their guns as I know we would have no hope if they surround us. They could, with their new rifle fire at us from two hundred yards at the firing rate of over twenty shots a minute, so we cannot wait for the other group of traps who are on the way to get here.

I goes over me plan again and again making sure I have thought of all the probabilities and how to handle them. I keep hoping that the traps will not fight when I tell em to bail up. Then I half doze, and half dream, and an image of Dan laying shot keeps coming into me dream. I wakes after a few hours and I relieves Joe Byrne from his watch, and I tells him not to wake Dan as I will do his turn so he is fresh for the morrow.

I feel uneasy as I watch the sun rise, and listen to the last call from the mopoke who had been calling all night, to be taken over by the laughing of a pair of kookaburras and the all too familiar warbling's of several magpies. I am suddenly at peace with meself and nature and feel ready. I prays again then head down from me little hill, to join Joe Byrne who is getting tea and damper ready. Joe is still moody and not very talkative, but I gets him talking and he tells me that we are dead men today.

THE SPIRIT OF NED

'I don't think so Joe,' I tells him. 'We have surprise on our side and we'll be in close before they know we are there, so snap out of it mate or you will not be any good.' Dan now comes awake, as does Steve and both look ready to go. After we've all finished our tea I tells em I am proud of em and then we mount up ready to do what we have been forced to do. Dan tells us that he hopes Fitzpatrick is one of the traps here and I tells him that I also do, and I says that I hopes Flood is one too. I looks at the boys with their bright sashes round their beltline, and with their hat straps under their noses, and I says a silent prayer for their safety. Ma's image now comes to me and I hopes she is alright.

We rides quietly to within a few hundred yards of where the traps were camping last night, and sure enough as we creep closer there is movement at the site. I can see only two traps, so we watch for a few minutes but it looks like Flood and Strahan are the only ones in camp. What luck, I thinks, the others must have gone looking for us, and now, I thinks is the right time to disarm these two. I signals to the others to creep closer, then I recheck me Enfield is loaded, and I steps out of the thick spear grass and give the two unsuspecting traps their chance to surrender. 'Bail up,' I yells. Joe Byrne with no weapon other than a blanket covered stick to make it appear like a rifle, tells em to 'throw up your hands.' Doing as he is told, Flood puts his hands as high as he can, and he is visibly as scared as a frightened rabbit. But Strahan runs for cover near where Dan has appeared with his pistol at the ready. Strahan dives behind a log, then reappears with his rifle pointed towards me brother,' shoot the mongrel,' Joe yells to Dan. But Dan could not pull the trigger.

I without thinking, and seeing the trap was about to shoot Dan, takes me attention from Flood and fires at Strahan from about forty yards. I knew if I missed him Dan was a dead man. I did not miss. The bullet hit him in the eye and he was dead. I quickly pulls me pistol and runs to Flood 'don't move' I tells him then I see he is not "him." 'You aren't Flood,' I tells him. 'No, I'm McIntyre,' he blurts out. Then he stammers out, 'and you just made Mrs Lonigan a widow.'

So I had not shot Strahan and this trap was not Flood. I tells McIntyre I'm sorry I had to shoot Lonigan. Me brother comes nearer and says that if Lonigan had of bailed up when told to he would be alive now, and furthermore, if he had not shown his intention to shoot us then he would not have had any trouble. Dan then got Lonigan's Webley pistol and ammunition. I Tells Steve, Joe and Dan to collect all the guns and ammunition. Joe Byrne asks McIntyre where the Spencer rifle is and he is told that officer Scanlon has it, and him and Sergeant Kennedy are looking for us lot now. 'Looking to shoot us in cold blood you mean' says Joe, who is now angry cause he has just looked in the traps tent and has found the "undertakers" or body belts that they had intended to strap our bodies on to their pack horses with. Joe kicks McIntyre in the knee and pushes him into the tent and tells him in his most snarly voice to throw the "undertakers" out.

Joe is now in a furious state, and as McIntyre pulls the terrible looking leather body straps into the open area in front of the tent, Joe picks up a tomahawk from the traps heap, and is about to bludgeon McIntyre with it but I steps between em and tells Joe Byrne, that best friend or not, I would shoot him if he tries to kill the trap. Joe glares at me in a way that I have never seen him look before, but he must have realised I was serious so he takes his temper out on the body straps and chops em into little pieces. I realize that the other two traps could return at any time, so I thinks out a plan and tell the others.

We covers the body of the dead Lonigan quickly then get ready for the return of the other two traps. I tells McIntyre that when the others do return he is to sit on the log which is in the middle of their camp, and I tells him what to say to them, and I also tells him if he tries any tricks I will shoot him.

I gets Steve Hart to hide inside the tent with the traps captured shotgun, and Dan and Joe to hide in the spear grass with other guns at the ready. I lays behind the same log that McIntyre is sitting on and keeps an eye on him. We don't have to wait long as Kennedy and Scanlon rides in, looking as large as life and supremely confident.

McIntyre does as he is told and says in a loud voice, 'the Kelly's are here, and we are surrounded.' The two returning traps obviously do not believe him and they laugh loudly. 'They ARE here, throw down your guns,' yells McIntyre. I then stands up with me rifle ready, but Sergeant Kennedy was already pulling out his revolver, so I fires a warning shot. Then Dan, Steve, and Joe came out of hiding and starts yelling to the traps to lay down their weapons.

Scanlon decides to be a hero and stirs his horse into action and rides straight at me firing at me as he comes. Scanlon was firing the new spencer rifle but his aim was poor and I automatically fire back at him and he falls off his horse dropping his rifle as he falls.

Things were not going to plan, and the situation called for reaction, because the moment the two returning traps chose not to surrender when told to, the whole plan was changed. I'd just shot Scanlon, now as I turns me attention towards Kennedy, who I knew was a crafty, fearless warrior, I am momentarily distracted by two shots from the area where Scanlon fell. This distraction was caused by Joe Byrne finishing off Scanlon. It almost cost both Dan and meself our lives. Kennedy was fast and shoots Dan in the shoulder, then he takes a shot at me and

I feels the bullet go through me beard. While all these bullets are flying Constable McIntyre seizes his chance and jumps onto Sergeant Kennedy's horse and makes a bolt for it.

Kennedy now runs into the trees still firing wildly. I calls for McIntyre to stop or I'll shoot him. He does not stop and it would have been an easy shot for me, but I could not shoot him in the back. So McIntyre gets away. I quickly check that Dan is alright, and sees that it is only a flesh wound to his shoulder. So I picks up Scanlon's Spencer rifle and try to see if I can use it, but I gives up and chase after Kennedy, loading me own weapons as I go. I calls out to him to stop and give himself up and that no harm will come to him. 'There has been enough shooting,' I calls out. Me answer came in the way of a bullet through me hat. I now know that he is going to try and finish me off. I sees him sneak down an old miners tunnel, and as I carefully creep in after the big trap, I thinks I may have lost him, then I reckon me training with old Harry Power saves me life.

I sense more than actually hear Kennedy behind me, and as I turns, I instinctively move sideways just as he fires at me from only about twenty yards. His shot goes past me head and I fires from habit and reflex, and me bullet hits him in the chest and I thinks he is a dead man. But he must be tough cause he staggers then goes for cover again. I yells to him to yield but he hides behind a tree. As I move closer he comes out and I am sure he is about to shoot at me so I shoots him first.

I moves closer to Kennedy, but to me horror I sees his revolver, which I thought he had pointed at me, but it was several yards away from the big man. I realise then that he was probably not aiming at me but raising his arm, which I now sees is heavily covered in his blood, to surrender. 'I'm sorry I shot you,' I tells the fatally wounded trap. 'Here take me gun and shoot me,' I goes to give him me gun but he says to me, 'no I forgive you, and may God forgive you too.' I sits him up a bit and tries to ease his pain, but he tells me he is a dead man. Kennedy then asks me to get his pencil and notebook from his pocket, which I does and he scribbles a note to his wife, and gives it to me asking me to give it to her. I tells him that I would and he slumps back and I now am sure he is dead, but he opens his eyes and starts talking about his family.

I listen as Kennedy talks about how they recently lost their eleven year old son. 'I will soon to be seeing him in heaven Ned,' he says. He is now in too much pain and begs me to end it for him. Without thinking I puts the shotgun to his chest and as I am pulling the trigger he says 'God forgive you.'

Kennedy, probably the bravest man I have known is now dead, but if only he had given himself up earlier when I first told him to. His word still echo in me head. 'God forgive, God Forgive.' I goes back to the traps camp and tells Dan, Steve and Joe to collect all the trap's guns, ammunition and supplies and to load them onto the traps four pack horses. Then I takes a blanket and Kennedy's cape back and covers him.

It was with no glory in mind that I shot those traps at Stringy bark Creek that day, in every case I gave them, in fact, encouraged them to surrender. Me main objective was to get the new Spencer rifle off em so as to stop em from shooting us, as that is what they had openly bragged that they were going to do. They came dressed not as law officers, but were clothed as prospectors, or heaven forbid, bounty hunters, which as Joe Byrne said, they were.

So now with four rifles, two shotguns and four Webley revolvers and the four trap's pack horses loaded with supplies, I burns the traps camp and we goes back to our hut at Bullock Creek. We had not been there long when Tom Lloyd comes with more supplies. He helps me clean and bandage Dan's shoulder, which is only a flesh wound and I thinks it should be alright. Tom insists, after I tells him about the shootings, that he stands watch while we get some rest. We do this, and then I tells him to go and not be a part of us as he may be falsely implicated with us, and be hunted by the traps. Tom wishes each of us good luck and is away as I have told him to do. We, I know cannot stay either, as I reckon as soon as McIntyre gets to town all hell will break loose and there will be traps everywhere.

CHAPTER TEN

We Run We Hide

Our hut at Bullock Creek must have reckoned that its days were not yet numbered, because as I lights it to burn it down, the rains come, and no matter how many times I tries, it will not burn properly.

With pack horses in tow, and Tom Lloyd gone, we the Kelly Gang head off, knowing that there will soon be dozens of traps out hunting us. I had asked Tom to tell me family that I had only shot the traps in self-defence, and I was no murderer. I planned to head us up to New South Wales but the rain set in and made heavy going, and looked like flooding the Murray and its tributaries. At least the traps would not be able to follow our tracks in this heavy rain as it turned the ground to mud.

Dan was complaining that his wound was bleeding and was sore, but we kept on across the flats, and I gave thought to stopping at me sister's place to tend his wound, but I did not want her involved. So after we had crossed the Oxley flats I stops and makes a lean to type tent and we rest so we can tend to me brother.

While Dan was sleeping Steve Hart says that he reckons he might go to Sydney and stow away on a ship bound for America or Africa, cause he thought we were done for here. Joe Byrne laughs and says he couldn't go on a ship cause he would get seasick before the bleedin ship left the harbour. I says that I wants to help free me Ma before I even think about getting that far away.

The rain eases a little, so we starts off again, and after two days we comes to the flooded Ovens River. We make another camp there and I gets Joe Byrne to go to the Moons hotel and pay for a bottle of brandy, which picks Dan up a bit, so we pushes on to Taylors Gap where we crossed the river. Dan were now getting weaker and slumped forward onto his horses neck, so I rides alongside him to help support him. When we gets to Everton I wakes a Mr Coulson and pays him well for hot food and hot tea for us all. Mr Coulson even gets Dan a change of dry clothes and packs us food to take. I thanks him and says 'Ned Kelly I am.'

Mr Coulson says that he knew this and that I was already famous and there were many people in sympathy with the Kelly Gang. I gives up the idea of New South Wales and we heads for the high country around Beechworth. When we comes near Joe Byrne's friend's Aaron Sherritt's place we fires a few shots into the air and Aaron soon comes out. He took a look at me Brother Dan, and says 'I knows a good dry hideout near here, and if Dan's wound is not 'scarred' with a hot iron soon, bleeding gangrene will kill him.'

So we follows Sherritt to a cave where he had a big pile of dry firewood stored, and he soon had a roaring fire going. We had a hot meal and plenty of hot tea which seemed to pick Dan up. But Dan's mouth dropped when he saw Aaron Sherritt pull a red hot iron bar from the fire. 'Take your coat and shirt off me boy,' he says to Dan.

Well me little Brother snaps back at Sherritt, 'me names Dan, Dan Kelly, and I'll thank you not to call me your boy Aaron bloody Sherritt.' Dan put on this brave act but he was near frightened to death of this hot iron.

Dan turns to me, 'Ned if I has to have it, then I wants you to do the job.' I looks at his red infected wound, and takes me belt off for him to bite on, then I grabs this hot iron and under the guidance of Sherritt, who is well known to be a bush doctor, I puts the thing against Dan's shoulder. I was proud as hell of me brother as he spat the belt from his mouth, and yelled 'Jesus,' then passed out and did not wake for about twelve hours, during which time we took turns at sleeping, with one of us always on watch.

Aaron Sherritt tells me that this is a safe place and there was no need to keep a lookout and that he would do so while we all slept. 'I have heard that you are in with the traps,' I tells him, 'and I thank you Sherritt for your help here today, but let me tell you one time only, if you dob on us to your mate Superintendent Hare, then you Sherritt is a dead man.' Sherritt backs away from me and says he won't do no such thing.

I am now not sure which way to go, so the next day with me brother much better, we heads back to cross the Murray River, but after three days of trying to get over the flooded torrent we gives up. As we pass through Everton again I knocks on the door of the hotel, and Mrs Vandenberg lets us in and I says we cannot pay her, but could we please have a feed, and if she would put it on the slate then Ned Kelly would see it right. Mrs Vandenberg looks at us all soaking wet and worn out, 'Come on in,' she says. I tells her I would be staying out here on the veranda keeping watch, but I would be obliged if she could feed me men. She does this then she brings me a feed of boiled potatoes and a big mug of hot tea.

I thanks this fine lady, and we are all feeling much better so we heads towards Wangaratta. As we pass the Delaney's house I sees Mrs Delaney pointing towards us and yelling and I knows she has recognised us and that she would tell the traps at her first chance. I leads me men right through the main street of this large town, then we cross the flats and onto the Mount Warby. We ride passing Steve Hart's place not daring to go in for fear the traps would be watching his and all our places. Then we sees the welcome sight of the bald hills knowing we were nearing the eleven mile and our country that we knew well and felt safer in.

I leads the way to Lake Rowan and Uncle Timothy's who I knew would feed us and give us supplies. Then I reckoned on moving back around Greta and the country that I felt I could outwit and outrun the traps much easier. Dan has improved rapidly, and as we ride towards me uncles place, Dan says in a whisper, 'we're being followed Ned.' I looks behind and sees a lone horseman about a mile back who is gaining on us, so we hide in a patch of thick scrub waiting in ambush for him. As he gets close I appears out from the scrub and tells him to bail up.

Steve Hart then comes out and the lone horseman greets Steve like a long lost friend. 'It's alright Ned, he's me old mate,' Steve says. They talks for a while and he gives Steve a bundle of supplies, then tells us that there is a trainload of traps at Beechworth and they plan to get the Kelly Gang. Steve's mate turns to me and says, 'can I join your gang Ned?' He goes on to say that he is a good shot and a trap hater, but I stops him short and tells him I thanks him for the supplies but he could not join us. He nods to me then passes some money to Steve, wishes us the best of everything, then rides off. I asks Steve Hart who he was as I had never seen this man before. 'He's a good friend of mine, and can be trusted,' Steve tells me.

We rides on to me Uncle Timothy's place and he puts us up for a few days, so we did not unpack the supplies given us by Steve's friend until we moved on. The first night after leaving me uncle's we made camp and I opens this parcel of supplies to find a rough note inside. I reads it out loud, 'Aaron Sherritt has dobbed you'se in and there is about thirty traps led by superintendent Sadleir himself following you.'

Well Joe Byrne goes off his head, storms about kicking everything, then says 'firstly he sleeps with me sister, then the traitor sleeps with the traps. Aaron Sherritt is a dead man,' Joe screams as he picks up the spencer rifle and goes to mount his horse. I reckons he is going to shoot Sherritt right now so I stops him and tell him it's not the right time with the traps everywhere, and that they were sure to be watching the mongrel's house. 'His day will come,' I tells him.

I leads us to us to a special hideout in the Warby Ranges called "Hells Hole." Me Sister Maggie knows this hideout and she, being a fine horsewoman, easily outrides and outwits the traps, to bring us supplies and news. Maggie first tells Dan and me that she has been to see our mother in the Melbourne gaol. 'How is Ma?' I asks. Maggie says Ma is doing alright and that she sends her love and that she knows her Neddie is not a murderer. Maggie says she has brought Ma's baby, me little niece Alice back to her place to look after her until Ma gets released.

Maggie is worried as she tells us that there is a reward of eight hundred pounds, dead or alive on the Kelly Gang. 'Ned they have passed a law which lets anyone shoot any of you.' Maggie then tells me that Patrick Quinn, Ma's brother in law has been very friendly towards the traps of late, and she is worried that he might be an informer. 'Tell Patrick that I'm on to him and if he is a traitor I will have to shoot him.'

Maggie stay a while and we talk a lot, about old times and then she tells me that this superintendent Sadleir is the very one who hired seven aboriginal trackers in Queensland recently, and they were successful in finding the people they were tracking, who were a group of aboriginals, 'and Ned they murdered all of them.' Maggie now tells me that Sadleir has the same seven trackers with him now and is planning to shoot the whole Kelly Gang. 'So, me brother, please be careful and look after our Dan like you promised our mother.'

Dan, who had greeted our sister earlier but then took his turn of guard, or watch duty, is now sitting alongside Maggie says, 'me lovely sister, let me remind you, in the good old Irish fashion that our mother taught us, and her mother taught her, that even though I'm a grown man now and capable of looking after meself, we look out for each other. So please tell our poor mother that we loves her very much, and yes Ned is looking out for me and I looks out for him.' I grins as Dan goes on with his chivalry.

He says, 'now me sister will you dance with me as we did when I was a child.' Maggie gets up and with tears in her eyes, she curtseys to Dan and they dance together a good old Irish Jig. Joe Byrne is on watch, so it's left to Steve Hart and meself to clap our hands to make the beat. We as is the custom, starts off clapping at the normal pace then gradually increase the tempo until Maggie and Dan are jigging and whirling at a tremendous speed. Finally Maggie is puffed and starts laughing, then she stops and drops her arms by her side and cry's openly.

Both Dan and meself gives her a hug then our sister asks if she may sing to us as she used to at home. I nod, as does Dan, and we sit back and listen to this wonderful, beautiful, sister of ours. Maggie has a beautiful rich voice and she starts off with The Black Velvet Band, and we all join and sing with her the chorus;

> *"And her eyes they shone like diamonds,*
>
> *I thought her the pride of the land;*
>
> *The hair that hung down to her shoulder*
>
> *Was tied back with a Black Velvet Band. "*

It was a fine time that we shared that day, and when we finished singing, I moves away a little to get us a feed and I can hear as Dan tells Maggie that he and Steve Hart are thinking of going to South Africa one day. I can see Maggie is not too happy with this news from Dan, and she shakes her head to him several times. We are sad to see our sister leave that day, but go she must. That night after me praying, I thinks how lucky and how good it is, that even after so much turmoil, so much hounding and persecution, that we are still a family.

A few weeks go by and its now mid-November Eighteen Seventy Eight and we are still hiding out in the Hell Hole, when I am on watch, and I sees the trackers heading straight to our hideout. I gets us ready, but I sees that there are only two trackers, and they were local boys. Jimmy was in the lead and I knew him and had in fact given his family meat from "borrowed" cattle on more than one occasion. Jimmy leans over the ground then points towards where we are waiting with loaded guns.

He leads about a dozen traps to within a hundred yards, and I knows he has seen me. Jimmy stares straight at me then touches his head ever so carefully so the traps don't notice. This is a form of sign language I take to mean, "I see you and all is well". Without any change in expression or movement which may alert the traps, Jimmy veers away and leads the traps well away from our hideout. I thinks that we must have some supporters out there, and feel a bit more confident about our chances of eluding the now two hundred traps, who according to Tom Lloyd, who had been to visit us, were out hunting The Kelly Gang.

We kept the Warby Ranges and Hell Hole as our main hideout, but as Dan and I knew the areas all around here, Steve Hart knew all the areas around his home country of Wangaratta, as Joe Byrne who hailed from the Woolshed district knew that area well, so we moved about and we kept a close watch on the traps. We had many, almost a dozen or so good hideouts and used them often.

We had an ever increasing number of sympathisers who either hid or delivered supplies to us and kept us in the news. Dan says to me one time as we kept an eye on a group of young traps who looked like they were just out of training school, 'look, they ride poor horses, they are poor bush men, they probably have never fired their rifles, and they are scared to come anywhere near where we might be.' We all laugh and I, on the spur of the movement, writes a letter which I gives to Maggie the next time she comes. I writes, 'Steele you mongrel, if you are still in my country in one month I'll get you.' Steele is one of the traps that has been annoying me sisters trying to find out where we are hiding out.

I rides back to the Everton Hotel one night and this big hotel owner answers the knock I gives his locked door, he looks at me with no fear in his eyes and asks who I was and what reason could I give him for knocking him up at this hour. 'I sir, am Ned Kelly and I've come to pay your good lady this here money for the feed and supplies she did give us a while back.' The mood changes and he shakes me hand then asks me in for a drink. 'No thanks I don't drinks much,' I tells him and I rides away.

Maggie tells me later that the story had spread right through the district and people are all saying that Ned Kelly is like Robin Hood. 'Cept he aint got a bow and arrow,' Joe Byrne laughs.

I now feels that we are safe and the traps will never catch us, but I reckon that as we are already treated as thieves, murderers and robbers we may as well act like them and rob a bank. We needs money for what we eventually plan to do. With this in mind we discuss which bank would suit us. It needs to be not too big a town, as there will be less Police to hinder us. After a few minutes Joe comes up with the very bank for us.

CHAPTER ELEVEN

EUROA

As planned, Joe Byrne, in early December in the year eighteen seventy eight, rides large as life down the main street of Euroa to check the place out. Joe goes into the hotel, a known place to gather information, and soon learns that a local lad named Bill George has passed away in an accident, and him being very popular, most of the town's population is expected to be at his funeral tomorrow, Tuesday afternoon. Joe talks to the manager of the De Boo's Hotel and gets as much information about the town as he can. He is offered a free drink, but declines and rides back to tell us all he has learned so we can plan our bank robbery.

After listening to Joe I agree that tomorrow afternoon is the time to make our move. Joe draws a map of Euroa, then shows us the bank and the Police station which is manned by only one Policeman by the name of Anderson. 'Good job, I tells Joe.' We gets ready and heads off towards Euroa, with the intention of camping somewhere closer to the town, and doing the job the next afternoon. We are in plenty of time, so as we comes the Faithful Creek homestead, I was feeling a bit hungry and we had plenty of time, so I leads us into the well-kept place hoping to get a good meal.

I tells the others to wait back a bit whilst I checked the place out. I knocks on the door and I smells the home cooking and I knows I have come to the right place. The lady of the house answers the door and tells me she is Mrs Fitzgerald, so I tells her me name is Ned Kelly and I would be obliged if me and me men could buy a meal of her wonderful smelling food. She calls her husband and repeats what I had told her. 'Well,' he says, 'if Ned Kelly has such good manners like he has shown, then give him and his men what he wants my dear.'

So we had a good feed and then I ask if the horses could be fed and stabled for the night. The stable hand, an uppity chap named Stephens tells me in a threatening tone that we could not stay there. He goes to walk away as though he had finished the subject, so I pulls me revolver and I calmly tells this little upstart, 'that we doesn't want to harm anybody, but if I must shoot somebody to get some service, then you Mr plumb in the mouth Stephens will be the first.' This changes his attitude and he promptly attends to our horses.

When he had finished, I takes him and a dozen or so other workers to a big wooden storeroom and locks em in. Mr Fitzgerald who had been quietly watching, then tells me that I cannot do this and that he won't stand for it, so I takes him to his storeroom and politely locks him in it too. I goes back to the main house where the boys are drinking hot tea, and I tells Mrs Fitzgerald that she and the other ladies and children must stay in the house, and if they do so then no harm will come to them. I then tells the ladies not to worry because the Kelly Gang are all gentlemen.

The night went quickly and the next morning the ladies prepared a huge breakfast of bacon and eggs with heaps of toast and honey, washed down with hot tea. I takes a huge tray of the same to the storeroom for me temporary prisoners, then we prepare to head to the bank at Euroa.

I leaves Joe Byrne to guard the Faithfull Creek Station, particularly the storeroom, but as we start to leave, four mounted men gallop up to us, but I'm ready for em and with Joe's help I puts em also in the storeroom. No sooner had we done this when Dan and Steve bail up a hawker with a cart load of goods that he sells to farmers and the like. Joe and I joins in and we all help ourselves to a new set of clothing, boots and all. Dan looks at himself in a mirror and says 'we sure look good.' There are now twenty two men locked in this very storeroom, and I tells Joe in front of em, before we go, to shoot any of em, that tries to get away.

Still we have one more task to do yet, I takes an axe from the farm and chops down the first seven telegraph poles, so no messages can be sent to the traps after our bank hold up. Now Steve Hart, Dan and meself finally go to Euroa. We travel to Euroa in convoy, we take the hawkers cart and use his young offsider as the driver, and I sits alongside him under the guise of being a gentleman going to the bank on business. Dan follows in a spring cart, and behind him is Steve on horseback. We must surely have looked the part of farmers off to town for the day.

THE SPIRIT OF NED

In me pocket I had a cheque for the amount of one pound and four shillings that I had got written out by the manager of the Station Mr Macaulay, who I had left alone in his own room in the Station house. I needed this cheque so that I had a reason for going to the bank.

The town was very quiet as we drove to the bank, probably because they were getting ready for the funeral. I gets out of the cart in front of the bank and tells the young driver to take the cart round the back of the bank, and I tells Dan and Steve to do the same, then I sets off to do me first bank holdup but the front door is locked, because of the funeral I thinks. So I knocks loudly on the door, and a young sounding clerk, without opening the door asks me what I wanted. 'I have a cheque to change,' I tells him. He tells me the bank is closed and he cannot open the door. I keeps knocking louder until he opens the door and starts to tell me that the bank is closed for the rest of this day, but he don't get the chance to finish as I pushes past him and shuts the door behind me. Then I pulls out me revolver, points it at him and says 'I am Ned Kelly.'

He is obviously no hero and puts his hands up in a flash. I ushered him, still with his hands near the ceiling, into the main bank area where a teller with a name tag of Edward Booth on his shirt is counting money. 'Bail up I says,' and when he sees me revolver his hands also brush the ceiling.

I moves now to the main office and reads on the door, "Robert Scott Manager", so I knocks on his door and enters. As most people full of importance do, he continues looking down at his paperwork on his desk. A little cough I gives, and as he looks at me I say, 'I'm Ned Kelly, so you bail up now.' He did so and I opens his drawer and takes his revolver out. Mr Scott did not raise his hand high like his two young employees, but Steve Hart comes in the back door with a pistol in each hand and the little manager quickly puts up both hands, very high.

I gathers up all obvious money while Steve enjoys himself pointing his pistols at his three prisoners. I knew there must be more money and I finds the strongroom, which is locked, so I asks Mr Scott for the keys. The silly little man refuses, so I goes next door to his wife and introduces meself and explain what had happened. Mrs Scott was very friendly and straight away produce a set of keys she says will open the strongroom. 'Well thank you Mrs Scott,' I says and we go back into the Euroa bank and I unlocks the big vault.

There to me delight was a nice stack of money, which I stuffs into me bag. I reckoned there was at least fifteen hundred pounds in me bag. Then I grabs some silver and over thirty ounces of gold, also three hundred pounds worth of sovereigns. There was a big stack of mortgages being held over the poor farmers properties so on the spur of the moment I takes them. We loads our small fortune and the Scott family and the two tellers into our borrowed carts and peacefully head back to the Faithfull Creek Station.

Joe Byrne had been left to guard the storeroom of prisoners which he had increased when a linesman had called at the station so Joe locked him up. So with our lot from Euroa we now has thirty seven in Mr and Mrs Fitzgerald's storeroom. I am happy with events, so after a cup of tea I opens the door of their makeshift gaol and tell them all that they could be free so long as they stayed within the house yard area. I says, with me pistol in me hand that if anyone tries to escape I would have to shoot them. They all agreed to behave, so after a nice meal provided by the ladies, I gets a bag full of bank coins and lets the children share em.

Then I invites em all into the big house for a sing song, which we all enjoyed. Then I tells all and sundry to come outside where I shows them the mortgages I had taken from the bank and then I burns them all. 'Tell these poor farmers that they now own their farms and don't have to pay the bank any money. Tell these people that Ned Kelly likes the poor farmers, and tell em how his poor Ma, who is a poor farmer, is falsely locked up,' I says.

Then Dan and me put on a trick riding show while Steve Hart stands watch. Dan really likes this "show riding," and is quite a star, and gets great applause from the now happy station people. Me Brother who I can remember teaching to ride, is probably the best horseman in the district, and I have told him many times this fact. He could have been, and may still go on to be a professional horse breaker.

We had just finished when I hears a train whistle and I thinks that it may the traps, so we get ready but only one man approaches and he is only looking for the linesman Mr Watt, who is in the crowd, but I tells the man from the train that Watt has gone on to Euroa. He leaves, so I goes back to the crowd of ex-prisoners and tells them that we had a good time, and I tells em thank you for the food and hospitality, then I pays Mr and Mrs Fitzgerald for this.

Then I says 'we are leaving and if anyone makes a move to tell the traps about us within the next three hours, I will come back and I will shoot them.' We gallops off a bit then I calls a halt and tells Steve and Joe to head off in one direction, and that Dan and I would meet em back at the hideout. Just to make it even harder for the traps to follow us I lets twenty or so station horses out and gallops em round and round in ever increasing circle, to cover our horse's tracks. Dan enjoyed this and was hooting and yelling like a cowboy.

We makes it back to camp alright and Steve Hart and Joe Byrne have already got the evening meal almost ready, after which we counts up the money from the bank.

That night Maggie brings us supplies and I gives her some money to be divided up amongst our families. Me Sister gives Dan and me a big hug, and says she will buy some clothes for all the families' children, and, she says 'I will tell them that their wonderful Uncles bought these clothes for them.'

We moved to different hideouts every few days after Euroa, to keep ahead of the traps, and one time Maggie brings some newspapers to read and I reads em out,

"Kelly Gang Again."

"Bank Robbed In Broad Daylight." "Re-appearance of the Kelly Gang." The Melbourne Herald went on to rubbish the police, saying that there were nearly a hundred police in the Kelly hideout area looking for them and don't seem to be getting the job done. It went on to say that any real bushman must be smiling at the way this Kelly Gang could just disappear at will.

The Herald newspaper interviewed the manager of the Euroa bank and Mr Scott said that, 'Ned Kelly was good looking fellow and a splendid specimen of the human race. At no time did he or his men harm anyone and in fact all the hostages at Faithfull Creek Station were in awe of the Kelly Gang.' This same newspaper went on to report that in response to the criticism, Captain Standish is moving his headquarters to Wangaratta.

Maggie tells me that I was now a legend amongst the common people and that I had thousands of sympathisers who were sending false reports of sightings of us to the traps just to put em on the wrong track. Some even dress like us, and some go as far as riding similar horses to ours and ride openly past traps and even police stations.

Maggie says there have been reports to police stations of sightings of us at Benalla, Beechworth, and Echuca, all in the same day. Some reported sightings said that they had seen the Kelly gang back in Euroa.

CHAPTER TWELVE

Desperate Men

At times Maggie would leave our supplies and sometimes a note at designated drop off places, and one time we got a note telling us that Captain Standish had asked for and got Superintendent Francis Hare along with his hand-picked troop of over fifty men and officers. Hare, the note says, is intent on taking the Kelly Gang "dead or alive." Hare is one of the most hated of all the traps and is known to have said he is after the reward money.

Also along with now over two hundred traps, seventy soldiers have been sent to Kelly country. Our sympathisers give em hell with their antics of false reports and dressing like us. Wild Wright gets arrested one time cause a troop of young "recruit" soldiers thought he was me. One such note tells us that Maggie and Tom Lloyd had been allowed to visit Ma, and though she was well Ma said she was worried that the traps were going to murder her sons. Ma told me sister that she prayed for us every night. Dan got quite upset on reading this and again tells me that we should leave the country before they buries us in it. I takes me brother aside and I swears an oath that I would help him to get away if things got too bad.

One newspaper clipping that Maggie left said that most of Victoria is now "Kelly Country," and another called northern Victoria "Kellyfornia." I had still an idea that someone in the position to be able to help us might do so if I was to write my feeling and appeal to him or her. But who? Joe Byrne suggests Mr Don Cameron, a local politician, so I gives Maggie this letter for him. I writes,

'Dear Sir,

Take no offence if I take the opportunity of writing a few lines to you wherein I wish to state a few remarks concerning the case of trooper Fitzpatrick against Mrs Kelly, W Skillion, and W Williamson, and to state the facts of the case to you. It seems impossible for me to get any justice without I make a statement to some one that will take notice of it as it is no use in me complaining anything that, she said the police may choose to say or swear against me and the public in their ignorance and blindness will undoubtable back them up to their utmost.'

I writes twenty two pages to this man in the hope of clearing our names. In me writings I tells how I had no choice but to shoot them. I finishes me letter by telling him that if he does not heed me letter and show some lenience to me mother by letting her free I would oppose his laws in many ways. I tells him that I have many sympathisers and I needs no lead or powder to revenge me cause, and if words be louder, I would oppose his laws with help. I signs off with,

'With no offence,

Remember your railroads,

And a sweet goodbye from,

Edward Kelly, a forced outlaw.'

Well after a week or so Maggie tells me that the Melbourne Herald did publish a bit of me letter. But, she said, Mr Cameron had firstly given me letter to premier and chief secretary Berry, who did not let the important parts be seen by the public. I do not take this very well and I reckon that there is no sense of justice to be had peacefully.

Me letter in fact seemed to have the opposite effect, as soon after receiving it Premier Berry orders warrants to be written for any, and all Kelly Gang sympathisers. Maggie tells me that already they have locked up Wild Wright, John Hart, Henry Perkins, Robert Miller, Dan Delaney and Jack Lloyd. The charge they trumped up was 'aiding and abetting' the Kelly Gang and when I was told this I sends money to employ the best defence for them. Me friends and relly's is still locked up and it's now the end of January eighteen seventy nine, and I am at a loss as what to do next to try to help them so I sends a letter to the acting chief secretary Sir Bryan O'loghlen, and with Joe Byrne's help I writes,

'Sir,

I takes the liberty of addressing you with respect to the matter of meself, me friends, Steve Hart and Joe Byrne, and me Brother Dan. I takes this opportunity to declare most positively that we did not kill the policemen in cold blood as has been stated by that rascal McIntyre. We only fired upon them to save ourselves, and we are not cold blooded murderers as we are made out to be. Circumstances have forced us to become what we are- outcasts and outlaws, and as bad as we are, we are not as bad as we are supposed to be. But, me chief reason for this is to tell you that you are committing a manifest injustice imprisoning so many innocent people just because they are supposed to be friendly to us. There is not the least foundation of the charge 'aiding and abetting' us against any of them, and you may know this is correct, or we would not be obtaining our food as usual since they have been arrested. Your policemen are cowards-every one of them. I have been riding with one party of them while they searched for me. I did ride with them for two hours, and they did not know me. We are desperate men, and we are determined men, and I want you to know that within a week we will leave your colony, but we will not leave it until we have made the country ring with the name "Kelly" and we have taken terrible revenge for the injustice and oppression we have been subjected to.

Beware for we are desperate men,

Edward Kelly.'

All this letter seemed to do was frighten the guards at Beechworth gaol into replacing the main wooden gates with metal ones, and they doubled the guards when they moved any sympathisers to or from any court hearings. These guards even had bayonets fixed at these times, so scared they were that the "Kelly Gang" would try to break their friends out.

It did seem that me letter may have stirred the newspapers a bit, as the Ovens and Murray Advertiser printed that the state of Victoria was in a sorry state of affairs, stating that there was no money anywhere, the government were communist and there was still a group of outlawed ruffians at large despite the hundreds of police and paid trackers out looking for them. It were common knowledge now, that Aaron Sherritt is giving information to the police, in particular to superintendent Hare. Sherritt tells them that he can lead them directly to us. Well, knowing this about the traitor Sherritt, I decides to move our main camp and hideout area.

Then Joe Byrne suggested that we should rob another bank. Dan joins in and says we might as well as our money is getting low, and we are already in trouble and have nothing to lose. So early in February, myself and Joe Byrne did call in to the Woolpack Inn which is a couple of miles from a town I thinks is ripe for the "picking".

CHAPTER THIRTEEN

Jerilderie is ours

Joe and I had a drink or two at Woolpack Inn, and the friendly barmaid subconsciously gave us a lot of information about the town of Jerilderie. I was very confident we would not be expected at Jerilderie as I had asked Maggie to spread the word mainly by telling Aaron Sherritt that we were heading to Goulbourn to do a job. I knows Sherritt would pass this information on to Hare and the traps would be expecting us at Goulburn. This "snare" I set would prove that Sherritt was the informer.

So Joe Byrne and me rides away and re-join Dan and Steve, and as I looks at em I smiles and thinks, so this is the feared Kelly Gang. Outlaws and murderers they calls us. But I know I am not, and nor are they. We were hunted and hounded by those traps that we shot, and they had full intentions of shooting us. They had bragged to me family they were going to do as much. Why as Joe had said, did they bring four spare horses and body straps if they did not plan to just shoot us? Yes they were in fact going to commit murder, as all we had done was to protect our sister and mother from the lying Fitzpatrick.

No, me conscience is clear, I had told em to bail up but they had killing us so much on their minds that they automatically tried to do this. Damn that lying mongrel Fitzpatrick I ponders. If only he were a man and told the truth about that night when he came to our house to annoy me sister. He used the story about Dan being 'wanted,' for an excuse, when he did not even have a warrant. Me Ma only clouted him on his helmet, and if he could have been seen by those who have judged us so quickly, when he was fondling me sister, and when he was told to stop by Ma, he laughs and would not stop and although already quite drunk he grabs another drink.

So Ma had no choice but to discourage him. If only the righteous bastards who locked me Ma up, if only they could see the drunken swine hiding behind his uniform try to shoot me Ma with his revolver, and if it were not for Dan, rushing and wrestling him to the ground, then the bullet he intended for Ma might have found its target.

Believe me, if this had of happened I would have shot this Fitzpatrick as sure as me mother come from Ireland. Yes if only they could have seen the coward grovelling and pleading when I did come in to find me brave brother wrestling him and trying to take the revolver from his hand, if only they could have heard him crying and swearing that he was sorry and that it was his fault and he would not report or ever say anything about this night. If this excuse for a man did not lie, then we would not be the "Kelly Gang," and we would not be on the run, and more so, there would be no dead Police.

Persecuted is what we were and always have been, and forced to be outlaws by those overconfident, scheming people who have hidden behind the thing that people fear and disrespect, the thing that they call the Law. Their law is not as it should be. Superintendent Hare told me sisters that he would see me dead, and that he was going to get paid a big reward for doing so.

I looks again at me "gang," Steve Hart, Joe Byrne, and me brother Dan, only just old enough to be called a man, and I was about to say I'm sorry for them being forced to become outlaws with a price of eight thousand pounds on our heads, but before I does, Dan snaps me out of me pensive mood by saying 'no time for dreaming big brother, we've a bank to rob.' Steve Hart, Dan's best friend laughs and me mood is broken, and so a merry gang sets off towards Jerilderie.

As we ride into town I remembers all the things about the place that the barmaid back at the Davidson Woolpack Inn told me. I also remembers how Joe Byrne was smitten by the barmaid there, and I had trouble getting him to leave the place. About midnight it is as we reach the front of George Devine's house. He is the senior policeman at Jerilderie, and I yells for him to come quickly as there is a riot going on out at the Davidson's place. I can hear the man stirring and mumbling so I yells 'hurry please, there is probably a murder there already. I think you better bring your constable with you sir.'

I remembers that the Constables name is Richards, so I asks them if there is only the two of them to handle this riot. Devine looks at me and growls out that the two of them can sort out any troublemakers alright. I pulls me revolver out and says to him 'can you handle this then?' They both look like they might go for their guns so I yells in me loudest voice 'I'm Ned Kelly and you better throw up your hands.' With guns in hands Dan, Steve, and Joe then come into full view and the two policemen lose their appetite for a shootout and real quickly both raise their hands high.

I am so relieved that they did bail up, because I did not want to shoot them. The officer in charge, Devine is looking real down in the mouth now, and he stammers out to me, 'my police career is now ruined by you Ned Kelly.' Dan looks at him and laughs as he tells him he would be better off with an honest job anyway.

We were all surprised when an obviously pregnant lady runs out and pleads with me not to shoot her husband. 'Which one of these gentlemen is he then?' It is obvious that she is Mrs Devine, but she points to him anyway, so I motions to Devine that it's alright for him to go to her, which he does and puts his arm around her. 'No Mrs Devine,' I says, 'I won't harm your husband, provided you all do as I say and do not try to raise the alarm.' We then take the two policemen to their own lockup, only to find that there is already a drunk in the cell, but we locks Devine and Richards in the same cell anyway. I then tell Devine that he has my word that if they all co-operate then no harm will come to his family. He looks me in the eye and says, 'thank you Ned.'

Into the house we now go where Mrs Devine introduces herself as Mary, then I introduces us to her. Mary Devine then cooks us a fine meal after which I tells her 'thank you,' and I says she may go to her bedroom until morning and no harm will come to her. The very pregnant lady takes her two children, and goes to her bedroom, knowing that she is safe.

The Kelly Gang then gets a few hours' sleep, but as usual one of us stays on watch. Early next morning Dan and I go and put on the two police uniforms and their guns, while Joe and Steve escort officers Devine and Richards into the kitchen where Mary Devine has prepared bacon, eggs, toast and plenty of hot tea. I watches while she serves the plates out to each person, then I swaps the plates around just in case. Well to be sure as me folks were Irish the look on the two policemen faces was truly a blessing when they saw Dan a meself sitting there dressed in their uniforms.

We takes the two officers back to the cells and then Mary tells me that today is Sunday and every Sunday she does the flowers in the church and she thinks that if she does not do them today then someone may think something is wrong. I tells her that she is right to mention this, and I gets Dan to escort her to the church while she does the flowers. Me brother thought he was top dog escorting a lady to church dressed in this police uniform, and I smiles and thinks, if only Ma could see her Dan right now.

Then it grabs me right in the chest as I remember poor Ma is still locked up unjustly. I am hoping that the letters I have been sending will get Ma an early release.

Well Dan brings Mary Devine back with no trouble, and I then sends Steve and Joe to escort constable Richards for a patrol, with the three of em dressed out in full police uniforms, except Richards has a revolver without any bullets. I tells Richards that the boys will promptly shoot him if he tries anything and he nods his understanding of the situation. 'Tell anyone interested that there are new police in town,' I tells him. I had told Joe and Steve already that they should check out the bank on the way round. All went well when the trio of "cops" returned, and Joe and I then had a good going over our plan for tomorrow's bank raid.

Dan and I then fed and groomed our horses, and Dan says he is pleased that we brothers are alone because if I did not mind, he said he had something important to ask me. I tells me now very serious brother to speak freely and that I would respect his question, whatever was on his mind. Dan is a bit nervous which is not like me brother so I asks him what is bothering him.

'Ned,' he starts off, 'I've been thinking, and I reckon it's only a matter of time before the traps nail us. So Steve and I reckon we might make a bolt for it soon.' I looks at me little brother and me mind goes back to when we used to play the things that we are now really doing, and how we used to wrestle, and ride, boy how we used to ride together for hours on end. I remembers teaching him not only to ride, but to be able to ride through thick bush at full gallop, and still be able to fire a rifle accurately. I thinks back to him trying on me hand me down clothes which were way too big for him, and how if anyone teased him he would fire up and fight anyone no matter that they were sometimes twice his size and if I tried to step in to give him a hand he would tell me to 'piss off, I'm doing alright,' even if he was getting a flogging.

I remembers one time in Beechworth I thinks it was, Dan was going to take on four big shearers who had been drinking a bit and were picking on him, and he was only about fifteen, and as luck had it I happened to walk in just in time to see these four ratbags in a circle round me brother. 'Need any help Dan?' I asks. Normally he would have told me to piss off, but he must have thought that the odds were stacked a bit too high against him this time, so he says with a grin 'just this once Ned.'

So outside we goes and Dan and I stand together ready to take on these four big shearers but they runs like rabbits. Then me brother chases em yelling that he doesn't blame them for being cowards cause nobody can stand up to the Kelly brothers.

This was about the time I had fought for the Victorian bareknuckle title and I guess they must have had second thoughts that day. Anyway Dan reckons he chased em away and nobody could tell him any different. I am snapped back to the present by Dan saying 'what do you think Ned?' I grabs him by both shoulders and tells him that if that's what he really wants then it's alright by me. I then asks him when they think they might go, and he replies that they want to see this through first.

We leave it at that and go inside where Joe Byrne is still writing me letter which I had now planned to ask Mary Devine to try to get printed in the local newspaper. Joe and I work on this letter which is more advanced than me one to Mr Cameron. Its fifty six pages that Joe and I have now bundled up ready to try to get printed.

I gets Dan and Steve to let the two police officers out, under escort for a bit of exercise while Joe and I go over tomorrow's plan one more time. That evening, after a good meal, Joe Byrne decides he wants to pay the barmaid back at the Davidson's Inn a visit. I tells him alright but not too much drinking.

I stays up late that night reading me letter to Mary Devine who does not show much interest, and when I asks her if she will take it to the newspaper's office to get it printed for me, she declined saying that her husband being a Policeman would not approve of her doing so. Mary tells me that a Mr Samuels might be the person I needs to see to have me letter printed. Joe Byrne comes home from his night out with Mary the barmaid, and I am pleased to see he is not drunk. He tells me he had a good night, then he promptly goes to bed, and I do the same. We all wake early and have a good breakfast on behalf of Mary Devine, after which Dan takes breakfast into the three cellmates.

It is still early so Joe and I read me eight thousand word letter. Joe stops me when we gets to "what would England do if America declared war and hoisted a green flag as it is all Irishmen that has got control of her forts and batteries?" Joe says that it is sounding like we are going to cause a revolution here in Victoria, and I tells him that it may well come to that if the system here does not change so the ordinary man can have a fair chance and not be persecuted and downtrodden all his very life. The time goes fast, and I think all is as ready as can be, so I stands up to me full six feet in height. 'Well,' I says, 'let us "Kelly Gang" give em something here in Jerilderie to remember, and get us a little money to fund the rights of our families and sympathisers.' Dan and meself dress out in full police uniform, while Steve and Joe are in their usual clothes. I plan to take constable Richards with us so as not to raise suspicion at the bank, so I tells him to wear his police uniform, gun and all, but with no bullets in it.

We leaves senior constable Devine locked in the cell with the drunk, and I tells Mary Devine that if she tries to raise the alarm then I would shoot her husband. We are now ready. But before we gets to the Bank of New South Wales I gets an idea. As we get near the Royal Mail Hotel I tells em of me new plan. Dan laughs so I know he likes it, so into the hotel we go. I had already told Richards what to do and say, and he does just that. Richards introduces us. The grumpy looking landlord is surprised when after telling us that his name is Charlie Cox, Constable Richards points to me and says, 'and this Mr Cox is Ned Kelly.'

If I am any judge of men, or if there is any chance that I can read men's minds, then I reckon Charlie the publican is already counting the money he will make when he can say, 'The Kelly Gang were here in my pub.' Charlie starts to talk but I cuts him short by telling him that we is here on serious business and if he does not cooperate, or he so much as tries to sound the alarm to anybody, then I will use this here revolver, and I puts it right under his nose. 'I'll do as you want Mr Kelly,' he stammers out. I tells him we needs his biggest room, and it must be lockable. Charlie is now, though nervous, obviously enjoying himself. Probably the thoughts of his future fame keeping him keen. He promptly shows me the big parlour, which I note fits what I wants.

I nods to Dan and Steve, and as planned they go and take all of our horses to the back of the hotel, then they draw their revolvers and make prisoners of all the hotel staff and anybody they see, then they brings em all into the parlour which has actually two doors, so I gets Dan to guard one and Steve to guard the other. Both of em are inside the big room which now has twenty nine "guests" inside it. Joe Byrne calls out 'drinks for everyone, and Ned Kelly is paying.' So with Dan and Steve staying to mind the now merrily drinking "guests," Joe and I head for the bank. Me plan was for Joe, who is dressed in his normal clothes, to go to the back do of the bank and pretend he is drunk and get in that way. Joe liked this idea and was enjoying himself, and when he starts yelling and talking like he has been drinking all day, one of the bank clerks jumps up ready to chase this drunkard back out the door.

THE SPIRIT OF NED

'Whassya name?' Joe says to the irate clerk. 'My name is Edward Living and you have no rights to be in here,' yells the young clerk who doesn't notice that this "drunkard" is now smiling, and young Living just about wets himself when suddenly there is a revolver under his nose. 'This gives me my rights,' Joe Byrne laughs. Young Living nearly faints when Joe adds a bit more to his game. 'I am Ned Kelly,' he tells Living. As this is happening another teller comes back to see what all the noise is and he too is met with a gun pointed at him.

Living stammers out, 'he's NNNedKKKKelly.' The new teller puts his hands up and pleads with this Ned Kelly saying over and over, 'don't shoot.' Joe tells them to be quiet and to follow him, and they are soon in the hotel parlour drinking with the other "guests." I have allowed time for Joe to do his part, now I goes in through the main front door of the bank, only to find that there are no tellers, in fact there is nobody at all, so I calls out, but still there is nobody anywhere. I starts to look around the adjoining rooms and sure enough I finds the bank manager. In the bath. I laughs a bit, and he is about to go crook as he doesn't yet know who I am. So I tells him, and after finding out that he is in fact the bank manager John Tarleton, I tells him to get out now or I may have to shoot him and spoil a good bath.

He gets dressed and Steve Hart arrives back with teller living, who Steve says had been bragging that he was the head teller, so Steve thought he might be the one to open any locked vaults. Well Living finds us nearly seven hundred quid, but says Mr Tarleton has to open the vault. The uncooperative manager shakes his head, so I puts me revolver close to his face and tells him that if he doesn't open it right now I would shoot him. This does the trick and from the vault we gets another stack of money.

While Steve is counting both lots of monies I look for any documents that might free some poor people of debt if we burns them. I tells Steve to take all and sundry to the hotel, and I finds a nice set of clothes in Tarleton's room and changes from me police uniform into his expensive looking set. I am feeling good, and I heads back to the hotel to join what is now a noisy group of happy drinkers. As I enters, me old schoolmate and best friend, Joe Byrne jumps up on the bar and yells for silence, and seeing the pistol in his fist everyone goes quiet, to hear Joe say as he points to me, 'this here well-dressed gentleman is the "Ned Kelly" and he has just robbed your bank and burnt all the mortgages over your properties, so with the drinks that Ned Kelly has paid for, I proposes a toast to him.'

There is a roar and much cheering and someone asks if I could tell em me story if it pleases me to do so. I joins Joe on the bar and does tell em how me Ma is falsely locked up and I tells the merry group the whole happenings of the "The Kelly Gang." All is quiet now, but I'm finished and jumps down from the bar, only to see me brother Dan take me place and him and Joe starts a singing The Wild Colonial Boy and the whole parlour full of people is now singing, even constable Richards. It must have sounded like quite a party going on. I was thinking of leaving, which I tells Steve I was about to do, so I can try to find the editor of the Jerilderie Gazette so I can get me letter printed.

Then I notices two men on the veranda so I goes to investigate. I grabs the nearest one and asks him where I can find Mr Samuels the newspaperman, and seeing me pistol he points to the other man and tells me his name is not Mr Samuels, its Samuel Gill. I turns to Gill but he up and runs like a rabbit. I know this Gill is too fast for me, so I figure this other chap must know where the rabbit has run to, so I grabs him to take him into the hotel with all the others. But he must be all of twenty stone in weight and it takes all me strength to get him inside the hotel where I asks him his name which he says is Hugh Rankin and he is just a storekeeper and he is not causing any harm and begs me not to shoot him. 'Then Mr Rankin, tell me where I can find this Mr Gill or I will shoot you.' I had just finished saying this when Steve Hart takes over and tells Rankin to get on his knees, then Steve cocks his pistol and holds it to the storekeepers head and tells him if he don't tell Ned Kelly what he wants to know then he is now a dead man. 'I don't know Mr Kelly,'Rankin cries. To the rescue comes constable Richards by saying he can take me to Gill, so I tells Steve Hart to keep up the good work and guard everyone, and I wink to Dan and tells him to keep buying drinks for all.

Constable Richards starts to take me to find this fast running newspaper editor then he suggests that we take the bank clerk, living, with us as he knows a bit about printing. So the three of us head off. Constable Richards takes us to the home of Samuel Gill, and I is met at the door by his wife. 'Don't be afraid,' I tells her. She says that she is not at all frightened but when I gives the letter to her and ask her to print it and get her husband to put it in the Jerilderie Gazette, she tells me no she won't do no such a thing for the Kelly Gang.

So I turns to Living and he shrugs and tells me that he would take a week to type it out, he said 'there must be over eight thousand words in this here letter you have done wrote.' Well I'm getting a bit upset and frustrated and I point me revolver at Living and tells him that I am leaving this here letter in his care and if he does not get Mr Gill to print it I would personally come back and shoot him dead. Seeing that the man is frightened enough by me threat, I gives him the fifty eight pages of me letter.

THE SPIRIT OF NED

Then I take all and sundry back to the hotel room and buys them a drink, after which I takes Joe Byrne who is still in his Police uniform and we heads for the telegraph office where we bail up Henry Jefferson and ask to see any telegraphs sent out over the last two days. None of them concerned us so we smash all the keys and anything that looks like a message sender. Then we takes him back to the hotel and they also take me free drinks quietly.

I picks out three big strong looking men and tells em I'll pay em each a quid if they will come and help me cut down about a dozen telegraph poles and cut up the wires, and I says 'if you don't then I will probably just shoot you.' They come quickly and we get the job done in no time. The men smile as I pays em and buys em another drink. The biggest of the trio, a man called Alan, says to me 'Mr Kelly, if you please, may I shake your hand and wish you well.' I shakes his hand and I am impressed by the strength he has. He tells me he is a boxer and he would be very happy to fight me for another quid. I looks at him and tells him that I would like very much to do so, but alas we must get away from here before the traps arrive. The big man nods and goes back to his drink, raises his glass and tells all in the hotel that he was drinking to the health of Ned Kelly and 'who in this room is going to do the same?' I was pleased when probably everyone in the room raises their glasses and says 'to Ned Kelly.'

I nodded to Dan Steve and, Joe and they make their way to me at the main door. Then I told Steve to get the horses. I then said to the crowd, who were all quietly watching us, that we The Kelly Gang were not murderers and we had no choice but to shoot those Police at Stringy Bark Creek as they were going to shoot us and in fact, had tried to do so. Then I said I would appreciate it if no one tried to get a message to the traps for at least twelve hours. I looked at them and then said that I would probably have to come back and shoot anyone that breaks this time limit I had politely asked for.

Then the four of us rides away, and as if someone, or something was watching, or as if we had ordered it, the rain came and washed away our tracks. We heads towards Deniliquin for a few miles then change direction but we let the Police horses that we had taken from the Police barracks stables go down the track towards Deniliquin. We had also taken all the Police guns and ammunition from Jerilderie as well as some horses. I later was given a copy of a message sent by post master Jefferson after we left Jerilderie, it read:

"The Kelly Gang stuck up the office here today at two o'clock, cut down the office connections and cut down seven poles. My assistant and I were covered by revolvers and were marched to the lockup, which The Gang had stuck up. We were there locked up together with two constables. We were released at seven pm and told not to touch the wire til morning, but I have done so and fixed a wire along the fence. They stuck up the Bank of New South Wales."

By now it is raining very much and I am thinking that luck is on our side for I reckon that soon the news will spread and hundreds of traps will be on our trail, but they will have their work cut out with our tracks getting nicely washed away. We ride by the bright moonlight all night and cross the Murray River just before dawn and we now feel much safer as we are nearing our "Kelly country." We make it back alright and it's not long before Maggie brings along with our supplies, some newspaper clippings, one of which was the Ovens and Murray Advertiser which had this to say, "The Kelly's have proved that truth is stranger than fiction, and their exploits read more like some eastern romance than a plain narration of what happened in Australia in the nineteenth century. Here we have the whole Police force of Victoria, which we had fondly regarded as one of the most efficient and best organised in the world, completely baffled, and defied by four youths, who exercised a terrorism which excesses even that of the bandits of Italy, and the pirates of Spain."

The story goes on how no one was harmed and how the Kelly Gang did again destroy many documents that the bank had as mortgages over many of the poor farmers. One newspaper even printed this song that was written about us, The Kelly Gang. It went,

"The bold Kelly Gang

Oh, there's not a dodge worth knowing

Or showing that's going

But you'll learn (this isn't blowing)

From The bold Kelly Gang".

Well it seems that the Kelly Gang are more famous than any bushrangers in Australian history so the newspapers say. I for one would swap any fame or anything to have me Ma released from prison. I am holding a hope that me letter I left in Jerilderie gets printed and the truth be known.

Maybe then they may look favourably at letting me poor Ma out of gaol. The reward on the Kelly Gang is now two thousand pounds each. Still, nobody who knows us and where we is at a certain time dobs us in.

CHAPTER FOURTEEN

The Letter

That letter it plays on me mind so much that it comes back to me in me dreams word for bleeding word, and it came to me this very night, and it was as if Joe was dictating it out aloud to me.

'Dear Sir,

I wish to acquaint you with some of the occurrences of the present, past and future.

In or about the spring of eighteen seventy the ground was very soft: A hawker named Mr Gould got his wagon bogged between Greta and my mother's house on the Eleven Mile Creek. The ground was that rotten it would bog a duck in places, so Mr. Gould had to abandon his wagon for fear of losing his horses in the spewy ground. He was stopping at my mother's awaiting finer or drier weather. Mr McCormack and his wife, hawkers also, were camped in Greta. The mosquitoes were very bad which generally are with a wet spring to help them. Mr. Johns had a horse called RotaCruta, which although a gelding was as clever as Old Wombat or any other stallion at running horses away and taking them on his beat which was from Greta Swamp to the Seven Mile Creek, consequently he entice Mr, McCormack's horse away from Greta. Mr, Gould was up early feeding his horses, heard a bell and seen McCormack's horse, for he knew the horse well.

He sent his boy to take him back to Greta.

When McCormack's got the horse they came straight out to Gould and accused him of working the horse, this was false, and Mr Gould was amazed at the idea. I could not help laughing to hear Mrs McCormack accusing him of using the horse after being so kind as to send his boy to take him from the RutaCruta and take him back to them. I pleaded Gould's innocence and Mrs McCormack turned on me and accused me off bringing the horse from Greta to Gould's wagon to pull him out of the bog. I did not say much to the woman as my mother was present, but the same day when me uncle was cutting calves, Gould wrapped up a note in a pair of the calves testicles and gave them to me to give to Mrs McCormack. I did not see her and gave the parcel to a boy to give to her when she would come. Instead of giving it to her he gave it to her husband. Consequently McCormack said he would summons me.

I told him neither me nor Gould used their horse. He said I was a liar and he could welt me or any of my breed. I was about fourteen years of age but accepted the challenge, and was dismounting when Mrs McCormack struck my horse in the flank with a bullock's skin. It jumped forward and my fist came in collision with McCormack's nose, and caused him to lose his equilibrium and fall prostrate. I tied up my horse to finish the battle, but McCormack got up and ran to the Police Camp. Constable Hall asked me what the row was about. I told him they accused me and Gould of using their horse and I hit him, and I told him I would do the same to him if he challenged me. McCormack pulled me and swore their lies against me.

I was sentenced to three months for hitting him and three months for the parcel, and bound to keep the peace for twelve months. Mrs McCormack gave good substantial evidence as she is well acquainted with that place called Tasmania, better known as Dervon or Van Diemens Land, and McCormack being a Policeman over the convicts and women being scarce released from that land of bondage and tyranny. They came to Victoria and are at present residents of Greta.

On the twenty ninth of March I was released from prison and came home. Wild Wright came to the Eleven Mile to see Mr Gunn, stopped all night and lost his mare. Both him and me looked all day for her and could not get her. Wright, who was a stranger to me was in a hurry to get back to Mansfield, and I gave him another mare, and he told me if I found his mare to keep her until he brought mine back. I was going to Wangaratta and saw the mare and caught her and took her with me. All the Police and Detective Berrill saw her, as Martin's girls used to ride her about the town during several days I stopped at Peter Martin's Star Hotel in Wangaratta. She was a chestnut mare, white face, docked tail, very remarkably branded (M) as plain as the hands on the town clock: the property of a telegraph master in Mansfield, he lost her on the 6th and gazetted her on the 12th of March. I was a prisoner in Beechworth Gaol until the 29th of March, therefore I could not have stolen the mare.

I was riding the mare through Greta. Constable Hall came to see me and said he wanted me to sign some papers that I did not sign at Beechworth concerning my bail bonds. I thought it was the truth. He said the papers was at the Barracks, and I had no idea he wanted to arrest me or I would have quietly rode away instead of going to the Barracks. I was getting off when Hall caught hold of me and thought to throw me, but he made a mistake and came on the broad of his back himself in the dust, The mare galloped away, and instead of me putting my foot on Hall's neck and taking his revolver and putting him in the lockup, I tried to catch the mare. Hall got up and snapped off three or four caps at me and would have shot me but the colt's patent refused. This is well known in Greta. Hall never told me he wanted to arrest me until after he tried to shoot me. When I heard the caps snapping I stood until Hall came close. He had me covered and shaking with fear, and I knew he would pull the trigger before he would be game to put his hand on me. I duped and jumped at him, caught the revolver with one hand and Hall by the collar with the other. I dare not strike or my sureties would lose the bond money. I used to trip him and let him take a mouthful of dust now and again, he was as helpless as a big goanna after leaving a dead bullock or horse.

I kept throwing him in the dust until I got him across the street to the very spot where Mrs O'Brien's hotel stands now. The caller was just dug then: there was some brush fencing where the post and rail was taken down, and on this I threw the big cowardly Hall on his belly. I straddled him and rooted both spurs into his thighs: he roared like a big calf attacked by dogs and shifted several yards of fence. I got his hands at the back of his neck and tried to make him let the revolver go, but he stuck to it like grim death to a volunteer. He called for assistance to a man named Cohen, and (Thomas) Barnet, Lewis, Thompson, Jewitt and two blacksmiths looking on. I dare not strike any of them as I was bound to keep the peace, or I could have spread those curs like dung in a paddock.

They got ropes, tied my hands and feet, and Hall beat me over the head with his six chambered Colt's revolver. Nine stitches were put in some of the cuts by Doctor Hastings, and when Wild Wright and me mother came they could trace us across the street by the blood in the dust, and which spoiled the lustre of the paint in the gate-posts of the Barracks. Hall sent for more Police and Doctor Hastings. Next morning I was handcuffed, a rope tied from them to my legs and to the seat of the cart and taken to Wangaratta. Hall was frightened I would throw him out of the cart, so he tied me while Constable Arthur laughed at his cowardice, for it was he who escorted me and Hall to Wangaratta. I was tried and committed as Hall swore I claimed the mare.

The Doctor died, otherwise he would have proved Hall a perjurer. Hall has been tried several times for perjury but got clear as there is no crime in the Police Force. It is a credit to a Policeman to convict an innocent man, but any mutt can pot a guilty one. Hall's character is well known about El Dorado and Snowy Creek, and Hall was considerably in debt to Mr. L O'Brien and was going to leave Greta. Mr. O'Brien seen no other chance of getting his money so there was a subscription collected for Hall. With the aid of this money he got James Murdoch, who was recently hung in Wagga Wagga to give false evidence against me but I was acquitted of the charge of horse stealing. On Hall and Murdoch's evidence I was found guilty and got three years' experience in Beechworth and Pentridge's dungeons. This is the only charge ever proved against me. Therefore I can say I was never convicted of horse or cattle stealing.

My brother Dan was never charged with assaulting a woman, but was sentenced to three months without the option of a fine, and one month and two pounds fine for damaging property by a Mr Butler, P M., a sentence there is no law to uphold. Therefore the Minister of Justice neglected his duty in that case, but three never was such a thing as justice in the English laws, but any amount of injustice to be had. Out of over thirty head of the very best horses the land could produce, I could only find one when I got my liberty. Constable Flood stole and sold most of them to the navvies on the railway line. One bay cob he stole and sold four different times. The line was completed and the men all gone when I came out, and Flood was shifted to Oxley.

He carried on the same game there. All the stray horses that was any time without an owner and not in the Police Gazette, Flood used to claim. He was doing a good trade at Oxley until Mr. Brown of the Lacrby Station got him shifted as he was always running his horses about. Flood is different to Sergeant Steele, Strachan, Hall and the most of the Police, as they have got hire cads if they fail, the Police are quite helpless. But Flood can make a cheque single- handed. He is the greatest horse stealer with the exception of meself and King George 1, I know of.

I never worked on a farm. A horse and saddle was never traced to me after leaving employment. Since February 1873 I worked as a faller at Mr. J. Sounder's and Rule's sawmills, then for each and Dockendorf. I never worked for less than two pound ten a week since I left Pentridge, and in 1875 or 1876 I was overseer for Saunder's and Rule, Bourkes Water-Hole Sawmills in Victoria. Since then I was at the Kings River. During my stay there I ran in a wild bull which I gave to Lydicher, a farmer. He sold him to Carr, a Publican and butcher, killed him for beef. Sometime afterwards I was blamed for stealing this bull from James Whitty, of Boggy Creek.

I asked Whitty in Oxley Racecourse why he blamed me for stealing his bull. He said he had found his bull, and never blamed me, but his son-in-law, Farrell told him he heard i had sold the bull to Carr. Not long afterwards i heard again I was blamed for stealing a mob of calves from Whitty and Farrell which I knew nothing about. I began to think they wanted me to give them something to talk about. Therefore I started wholesale and retail horse and cattle dealing. Whitty and Burns not being satisfied with all the picked land on the Boggy Creek and King River, and the run of their stock on certified land free and no one interfering with them, paid heavy rent to the banks for all the open ground, so as a poor man could keep no stock. They impounded every beast they could get, even off the government roads.

If a poor man happened to leave his horse or a bit of a poddy calf outside his paddock they would be impounded. I have known of over 60 head of horses impounded in one day by Whitty and Burns, all belonging to poor farmers. They would have to leave their ploughing or harvest or other employment to go to Oxley. When they would get there, perhaps they would not have money enough to release them, and have to give a bill of sale or borrow money which is no easy matter. Along with this sort of work, Farrell the Policeman stole a horse from George King and had him in Whitby's and Farrell's paddocks until he left the force. All this was the cause of me and my step-father George King taking their horses and selling them to Baumgarten and Kennedy.

The pick of them was taken to a good market and the culls were kept in Peterson's paddock, and their brands altered by me. Two was sold to Kennedy and the rest to Baumgarten who were strangers to me, and I believe honest men. They paid me full value for the horses and could not have known they were stolen. No person had anything to do with the stealing and selling of the horses but me and George King. William Cooke, who was convicted for Whitby's horses, was innocent. He was not in my company at Peterson's.

But it is not the place of the Police to convict guilty men, as it is by them they get their living. Had the right parties been convicted it would have been a bad *job for the Police as Berry would have sacked a great many of them. Only I came to their aid and kept them in their billets and good employment and got them double pay, and yet the ungrateful articles convicted my mother and an infant, my Brother-in-Law and another man who was innocent, and still annoy my brothers and sisters. The ignorant unicorns even threaten to shoot myself, but as soon as dead they will all be heels up in the maroon. There will be no more Police required. They will be sacked and supplanted by soldiers on low pay in the towns, and special constables made some of the farmers to make up for this double pay and expense.*

It will pay the Government to give those people who are suffering innocence, justice and liberty. If not I will be compelled to show some colonial stratagem which will open the eyes of not only the Victorian Police, and inhabitants, but also the whole British army. No doubt they will acknowledge their hounds were barking at the wrong stump, and that Fitzpatrick will be the cause of greater slaughter to the Union Jack than Saint Patrick was to the snakes and toads in Ireland. The Queen of England was as guilty as Baumgarten and Kennedy, Williamson and Skillion of what they were convicted for. When the horses were found on the Murray River I wrote a letter to Mr Swan hill of Lake Rowan to acquaint the auctioneer and to advertise my horses for sale. I brought some of them to that place, but did not sell. I sold of them in Benalla, Melbourne and other places, and left the colony and became a rambling gambler.

Soon after I left there was a warrant for and the Police searched the place and watched night and day for two or three weeks. When they could not snare me they got a warrant against my brother Dan, and on the 15th of April Fitzpatrick came to the Eleven Mile Creek to arrest him. He had some conversation with a horse- dealer whom he swore was William Skillion. This man was not called in Beechworth besides several other witnesses, who alone could have proved Fitzpatrick's falsehood.

After leaving this man he went to the house and asked was Dan in. Dan came out. I hear previous to this Fitzpatrick had some conversation with Williamson on the hill. He asked Dan to come to Greta with him, as he had a warrant for him for stealing Whitby's horses. Dan said "All wright", and they both went inside. Dan was having something to eat. His mother asked Fitzpatrick what he wanted Dan for. The trooper said he had a warrant for him. Dan then asked him to produce it. He said it was only a telegram sent from Chiltern, but Sergeant Whelan ordered him to relieve Steele at Greta, and call and arrest Dan and take him to Wangaratta next morning and get him remanded. Dan's mother said Dan need not go without a warrant unless he liked, and that the trooper had no business on her premises without some authority besides his own word.

The trooper pulled out his revolver and said he would blow her brains out if she interfered with the arrest. She told him it was a good job for him Ned was not there, or he would ram his revolver down his throat. Dan looked out and said, "Ned is coming now. " The trooper being off his guard, looked out and when Dan got his attention drawn, he dropped the knife and fork, which showed he had no murderous intent, and slapped Henan's hug on him, took his revolver and kept him there until Skillion and Ryan come with horses Dan sold that night.

The trooper left and invented some scheme to say that he got shot, which any man can see is false. He told Dan to clear out, that Sergeant Steele and Detective Brown and Strachan would be there before morning. Strachan had been over the Murray to get up a case against him, and they would convict him if they caught him as the stock society offered an enticement for witnesses to swear anything and the Germans over the Murray would swear to the wrong man as well as the right.

Next day Williamson and my mother was arrested, and Skillion the day after, who was not there at the time of the row, which can be proved by 8 or 9 witnesses. The Police got great credit and praise in the papers for arresting the mother of 12 children, one an infant on her breast, and those two quiet, hardworking innocent men who would not know the difference between a revolver and a sauce panhandle, kept them six months awaiting trial and then convicted them on the evidence of the meanest article that the sun ever shone on. It seems that the jury was well chosen by the Police as there was a discharged Sergeant amongst them, which is contrary to law. They thought it impossible for a Policeman to swear a lie, but I can assure them that it was by that means and hiring cads they got promoted. I have heard from a trooper that he never knew Fitzpatrick to be one night sober, and that he sold his sister to a Chinaman, but he looks a young, strapping rather genteel man, more fit to be a starcher to a laundress than a Policeman for the keen observer he has the wrong appearance for a manly heart. The deceit and cowardice is too plain to be seen in the puny cabbage-hearted looking face.

I heard nothing of this transaction until very close to the trial, I being 400 miles from Greta. I heard I was outlawed and a hundred pound reward for my shooting a trooper in Victoria and a hundred pound for any man that could prove a conviction of horse-stealing against me, so I came back to Victoria. I knew I would *get no justice if I gave myself up, I enquired after my brother Dan and found him digging on Bullock Creek, I heard how the Police used to be blowing that they would not ask me to stand; they would shoot me first and then cry surrender.'*

WAKE UP NED, and its Dan there shaking me then he grabs me arm to stop me pointing me pistol at him, 'Joe thinks someone is snooping close by Ned,' I must have been in a deep sleep cause I normally would have heard any noise before Joe or anyone, and quickly jump up and follow me brother to where can now hear Joe and Steve talking to someone and to me relief and great pleasure its dear Maggie with supplies. She doesn't stay long and as it is only about two in the morning we all go back for a bit more shut eye, all except Steve who stays on watch duty.

I find it hard to get back to sleep as I am thinking about this "Jerilderie letter" that I must admit that Joe Byrne did actually write mostly. I am now realizing that not all of the fact are true, as Joe's idea was to try to prove that I was not there when Fitzpatrick comes to me Ma's house that night, but I knows that I was and it is bugging me that there are some untruths in this letter. Finally I am drifting off to the land of nod and I must have picked up dreaming about this letter where I left off...

And how they used to rush into the house and upset all the milk dishes, break tins of eggs, empty the flour out of the bags onto the ground, and even meat out of the casks and destroy all the provisions and shove the girls in front of them into the rooms like dogs, so as if anyone was there they would shoot the girls first. But they knew well I was not there, or I would have scattered their blood and brains like rain. I would manure the Eleven Mile with bloated carcases, and yet remember there is not one drop of murderous blood in my veins.

Superintendent Smith used to say to my sisters, "See all the men I have out today? I will have as many more tomorrow and we will blow him into pieces as small as the paper that is in our guns. Detective Ward and Constable Hayes took out their revolvers and threatened to shoot the girls and children in Mrs. Skillion's absence. The greatest ruffians and murderers, no matter how depraved would not be guilt of such a cowardly action. This sort of cruelty and disgraceful and cowardly conduct to my brothers and sisters who had no protection, coupled with the conviction of my mother and those men certainly made my blood boil. I don't think there is a man born could have the patience to suffer it as long as I did, or ever allow his blood to get cold while such insults as these were unavenged. Yet in every paper printed I am called the blackest and coldest-blooded murderer on record. But if I hear any more of it

I will not exactly show them what cold blooded murder is, but wholesale and retail slaughter-something different to shooting three troopers in self-defence and robbing a bank. I would have been rather hot blooded to throw down my rifle and let them shoot me and my innocent brother. They were not satisfied with frightening my sisters night and day, and destroying their provisions and lagging my mother and infant, and those innocent men, but should follow me and my brother into the wilds where we had been quietly digging, neither molesting or interfering with anyone. He was making good wages, as the creek is very rich within half a mile from where I shot Kennedy.

I not there long and on the 25th of October I came on Police tracks between Table Top and the Bogs. I crossed them and returning in the evening I came on a different lot of tracks making for the shingle hut. I went to our camp and told my brother and his two mates. Me and my brother went and found their camp at the shingle hut, about a mile from my brother's house. We saw they carried long firearms and we knew doom was sealed if we did not beat those before the others would come. I knew the other Police party would soon join them, and if they came on us at our camp they would shoot us down like dogs at our work as we had only two guns. We thought it best to try and bail those two up, take their firearms and ammunition and horses, and we could stand a chance with the rest. We approached the spring as close as we could get to the camp, as the intervening space being clear ground and no battery. We saw two men at the logs. They got up and one took a double-barrelled fowling piece, and fetched a horse down and hobbled him at the tent. We thought there were more men in the tent asleep, and those outside being on sentry. We could have shot those two men without speaking, but not wishing to take their lives, we waited. McIntyre laid his gun against a stump and Lonigan sat on a log. I advanced, my brother Dan keeping McIntyre covered which he took to be constable Flood, and had he not obeyed my orders, or attempted to reach for the gun or draw his revolver, he would have been shot dead.

When I called on them to throw up their hands McIntyre obeyed and Lonigan ran some six or seven yards to a battery of logs, instead of dropping behind the one he was sitting on. He had just got to the logs and put his head up to take aim when I shot him that instant, or he would have shot me, as I took him for Strachan, the man who said he would not ask me to stand, but would shoot me first like a dog. But it happened to be Lonigan, the man who, in company with Sergeant Whelan, Fitzpatrick and King the boot maker, and Constable O'Day, tried to put a pair of handcuffs on me in Benalla, but he could not and had to allow McInnis the miller to put them on.

Previous to Fitzpatrick swearing he was shot, I was fined two pounds for hitting Fitzpatrick, and two pounds for not allowing five curs like Sergeant Whelan, O'Day, Fitzpatrick, King and Lonigan (who caught me by the privates and would have sent me to Kingdom Come only I was not read) to arrest me. He is the man who blowed before he left Violet Town that if Ned Kelly was to be shot, he was the man would shoot him. No doubt he would shoot me, even if I drew up my arms and laid down as he knew four of them could not arrest me single handed, not to talk of the rest of my mates. Either he or I would have to die. This he knew well, therefore he had a right to keep out of my road. Fitzpatrick is the only one I hit out of the five in Benalla: this shows my feeling towards him as he said we were good friends and even swore it. But he was the biggest enemy I had in the country with the exception of Lonigan, and he can be thankful I was not there when he took a revolver and threatened to shoot my mother in her own house.

It is not true I fired three shots and missed him at a yard and a half. I don't think would use a revolver to shoot a man like him when I was within a yard and a half of him, or attempt to fire into a house where my mother, brothers and sisters was, and, according to Fitzpatrick's statement all around him. A man that is such a bad shot as to miss a man three times at a yard and a half would never attempt to fire into a house among a houseful of women and children while I had a pair of arms and a bunch of fives at the end of them, and Fitzpatrick knew the weight of them only too well as it run up against once in Benalla and cost me two pounds odd, as he is very subject to fainting.

As soon as I shot Lonigan he jumped up and staggered some distance from the logs with his hands raised and then fell. He surrendered, but too late. I asked McIntyre who was in the tent. He replied. "No one. "I advanced and took possession of their two revolvers and fowling piece, which I loaded with bullets instead of shot. I asked McIntyre where his mates was. He said they had gone down the creek and he did not expect them that night. He asked me was I going to shoot his mates. I told him no: I would shoot no man if he gave up his arms and promised to leave the Force.

He said the Police all knew Fitzpatrick had wronged us, and he intended to leave the Force as he had health and his life was insured. He told me he intended going home, and that Kennedy and Scanlon were out looking for our camp and also about the other Police. He told me that the N.S.W. Police had shot a man for shooting Sergeant Walling. I told him that if they did they had shot the wrong man and I expect your band came to do the same to me. He said no, they did not come to shoot me, they come to apprehend me. I asked him what they carried Spencer rifles and breach-loading fowling pieces and so much ammunition for, as the Police was only supposed to carry one revolver and six cartridges in the revolver, but they had eighteen round of revolver cartridge each, tree dozen for the fowling piece and twenty one Spencer rifle cartridges, and God knows how many they had away with the rifle. This looked as if they meant not only to shoot me, but to riddle me, but I don't know either Kennedy or Scanlon or him and had nothing against them, as I could not blame them, they had to do their duty.

I said I did not blame them for doing honest duty, but I could not suffer them blowing me to pieces in my own native land. If they knew Fitzpatrick wronged us why not make it public and convict him, but no, they would rather riddle poor unfortunate creoles. But they will rue the day Fitzpatrick got among them. Our two mates came over when they heard the shot fired, but went back again for fear the Police might come to our camp while we were all away and manure Bullock Flat with us on arrival.

I stopped at the logs and Dan went back to the spring for fear the Troopers would come in that way, but I soon heard them coming up the creek. I told McIntyre to tell them to give up their arms. He spoke to Kennedy, who was some distance in front of Scanlon. He reached for his revolver and jumped off, on the offside of his horse and got behind a tree. When I called on them to throw up their arms, Scanlon, who carried his rifle slewed his horse around to gallop away but the horse would not go, and as quick as thought, fired at me with the rifle without unslinging it and was in the act of firing again when I had to shoot him, and he fell from his horse.

I could have shot them without speaking but their lives was no good to me. McIntyre jumped on Kennedy's horse and I allowed him to go as I did not like to shoot him after he had surrendered, or I would have shot him as he was between me and Kennedy. Therefore I could not shoot Kennedy without shooting him first. Kennedy kept firing from behind the tree. My Dan advanced and Kennedy ran. I followed him. He stopped behind another tree and fired again. I shot him in the armpit and he dropped his revolver and ran. I fired again as he slewed around to surrender. I did not know he had dropped his revolver- the bullet passed the right side of his chest and he could not live- or I would have let him go. Had they been my own brothers I could not help shooting them or else let them shoot me, which they would have done if their bullets been directed as they intended them.

But as for handcuffing Kennedy to a tree, or cutting his ear off, or brutally treating any of them is a falsehood. If Kennedy's ear was cut off it was not done by me, and none of my mates was near him after he was shot. I put his cloak over him and left him as well as I could, and were they my own brothers I could not have been more sorry for them. This cannot be called wilful murder for I was compelled to shoot them, or lie down and let them shoot me. It would not have been wilful murder if they packed our remains in, shattered us to a mass of animated gore to Mansfield. They would have got great praise and credit as well as promotion, but I am reckoned a horrid brute because I had not been cowardly enough to lie down for them under such trying circumstances, and insults to my people.

Certainly their wives and children are to be pitied, but they must remember those men came into the bush with the intention of scattering pieces of me and my brother all over the bush, and yet they know and acknowledge I have been wronged and my mother and four or five men lagged innocent. And is my brothers and sisters and my mother not to be pitied also, who has no alternative, only to put up with the brutal, and cowardly conduct of a parcel of big, fat necked, wombat-headed, big-bellied, magpie-legged, narrow-hipped, splay-footed sons of Irish bailiffs or English Landlords which is better known as officers of Justice or Victorian Police, who some calls honest gentlemen. But I would like to know what business an honest man would have in the Police, as it is an old saying, it takes a rogue to catch a rogue. And a man that knows nothing about roguery would never enter the Force and take an oath to arrest brother, sister, father, or mother if required, and to have a case and conviction if possible.

Any man knows it is possible to swear a lie, and if a Policeman loses a conviction for the sake of swearing a lie, he has broken his oath. Therefore he is a perjurer either ways. A Policeman is a disgrace to his country, not alone to the mother that suckled him. In the first place he is a rogue in his heart, but too cowardly to follow it up without having the Force to disguise it. Next, he is a traitor to his country, ancestors and religion, as they were all Catholics before the Saxons and Cranmore yoke held sway. Since then they were persecuted, massacred, thrown into martyrdom and tortured beyond the ideas of the present generation.

What would people say if they saw a strapping big lump of an Irishman shepherding sheep for fifteen bob a week or tailing turkeys in Tallarook ranges for a smile from Julia, or even begging his tucker? They would say he ought to be ashamed of himself and tar and feather hint. But he would be a king to a policeman, who for a lazy, loafing, cowardly billet left the ash corner and deserted the shamrock, the emblem of true wit and beauty to serve under a flag and nation that has destroyed, massacred and murdered their forefathers by the greatest of torture, such as rolling them downhill in spiked barrels, pulling out their toe and finger nails, and an the wheel and every torture imaginable.

More was transported to Van Diemen's Land to pine their young lives away in starvation and misery among tyrants worse than the promised hell itself. All of true blood, bone and beauty, that was not murdered on their own soil, or had fled to America or other countries to bloom again another day were doomed to Port Macquarie, Toongabbie, Norfolk Island and Emu Plains, and in those places of tyranny and condemnation, Manu a blooming Irishman, rather than subdue to the Saxon yoke, were flogged to death and bravely died in servile chains, but true to the shamrock and a credit to Paddy's Land.

What would people say if I became a Policeman and took an oath to arrest my brothers and sisters and relations, and convict them by fair of foul means, after the conviction of my mother and the persecution and insults offered to myself and people? Would they say I was a decent gentleman? And yet a Policeman is still in worse and quilt of meaner action than that. The Queen must surely be proud of such heroic men as the Police and Irish soldiers, as it takes eight or eleven of the biggest mud-crunchers in Melbourne to take one poor little half-starved larrikin to a watch house. I have seen as many as eleven, big and ugly enough to lift Mount Macedon out of a crab hole, more like the species of a baboon or gorilla than a man, actually come into a court house and swear they could not arrest one eight stone larrikin and them armed with battens and niddies. Without some civilians' assistance, and some of them going to hospital from the effects of hits from the fists of the larrikin, and the Magistrate would send the poor little larrikin into a dungeon for being a better man that such a parcel of armed curs.

What would England do if America declared war and hoisted a green flag, as it is all Irishmen that has cot command of her armies' forts and batteries? Even her very life guards and beef tasters are Irish. Would they not slew round and fight her with their own arms for the sake of the colour they dare not wear for years, and to reinstate it and raise old Erin's isle once more from the pressure and tyrannism of the English yoke, which has kept it in poverty and starvation and caused them to wear the enemy's coat? What else can England expect?

Is there not big, fat Unicorns enough paid to torment and drive me to do things which I don't wish to do, without the public assisting them? I have never interfered with any person unless they deserved it, and yet there are civilians who take firearms against me, for what reason I do not know unless they want me to turn on them and exterminate them without medicine. I shall be compelled to make an example of some of them if they cannot find no other employment. If I had robbed and plundered, ravished and murdered everything I me, young and old, rich and poor, the public could not do any more than take firearms and assist the Police as they have done, but by the light that shines, pegged on an ant-bed with their bellies opened, their fat taken out, rendered, and poured down their throats boiling hot will be cool to what pleasure I will give some of them. Any person aiding or harbouring or assisting the Police in any way whatever, or employing any person whom they know to be a detective or cad, or those who would be so depraved as to take blood money will be outlawed and declared unfit to be allowed human burial. Their property either consumed or confiscated and them, theirs and all belonging to them exterminated off the face of the earth. The enemy I cannot catch myself I shall give a payable reward for.

I would like to know who put that article that reminds me of a poodle dog, half clipped in the lion fashion, called Brooke E. Smith, Superintendent of Police. He knows as much about commanding Police as Captain Standish does about mustering mosquitoes and boiling them down for their fat on the backblocks of the Lachlan, for he has a head like a turnip, a stiff neck as big as his shoulders, narrow hipped and pointed towards the feet like a vine stake. If there is anyone to be called a murderer regarding Kennedy, Scanlon and Lonigan, it is that misplaced poodle. He gets as much pay as a dozen good troopers, if there is any good in them, and what does he do for it? He cannot look behind him without turning his whole frame. It takes three or four Police to keep sentry while he sleeps in Wangaratta, for fear of body snatchers. Do they think he is a superior animal to the man that has to guard him? If so, why not send the men that gets big pay and reckoned superior to the common Police after me and you shall soon save the country of high salaries to men that is fit for nothing else but getting better men that himself shot, and sending orphan children to the industrial school to make prostitutes and cads of them for the Detectives and other evil disposed persons.

Send the high paid and men that received big salaries for years in a gang by themselves after me, as it makes no difference to them, but it will give them a chance of showing whether they are worth more pay than a common trooper or not. I think the public will soon find they are not only in the road of good men but obtaining money under false pretences. I do not call McIntyre a coward, for I reckon he is a game a man as wears a Jacket, as he had the presence of mind to know his position directly he was spoken to, and only foolishness to disobey.

It was cowardice that made Lonigan and the others fight. It is only foolhardiness to disobey an outlaw, as a Policeman or other man who do not throw up their arms directly as I call on them, knows the consequences, which is a speedy dispatch to Kingdom Come. I wish those men who joined the stock Protection Society to withdraw their money and give it and as much more to the widows, and orphans and poor of Greta district, where I spent and will again spend many a happy day, fearless, free and bold, as it only aids the Police to procure false witnesses and go whacks with men to steal horses and lag innocent men. It would suit them far better to subscribe a sum and give it to the poor of their district, and there is no fear of anyone stealing their property, for no man could steal their horses without the knowledge of the poor.

If any man was mean enough to steal their property, the poor would rise out to a man and find them if they were on the face of the earth. It will always pay a rich man to be liberal with the poor and make as little enemies as he can, as he shall if the poor is on his side, he shall lose nothing by it. If they depend on the Police they shall be drove to destruction, as they cannot and will not protect them. If duffing and bushranging were abolished, the Police would have to cadge for their living. I speak from experience, as I have sold horses and cattle innumerable, and yet eight head of the culls is all ever was found. I never was interfered with whilst I kept up this successful trade.

I give fair warning to all those who has reason to fear me to sell out, and give 10 pounds out of every hundred towards the widow and orphan fund and do not attempt to reside in Victoria but as short a time as possible after reading this notice, neglect this and abide by the consequences, which shall be worse than the rust in the wheat in Victoria or the truth of a dry season to the grasshoppers in New South Wales.

I do not wish to fire the order full force without giving timely warning, but I am a widow's son outlawed, and my orders must be obeyed.

Edward Kelly.'

'Wake up Ned. Ned...wake up its bleeding eight o'clock. I now come out of a deep sleep and it's Dan who is laughing at me for sleeping so long. 'You must have been dreaming about your black haired beauty me brother, for the days half gone and we better move on.' Dan is joined in his mocking laughter by Steve Hart and Joe Byrne.

I gets up and grabs a bite to eat and we move on, and I make a point of riding close to Joe so as I can talk about how I kept dreaming about the "Jerilderie Letter" all night. I tells him that I now sort of hope that this letter does not get published as it is not one hundred percent true. I tells Joe that he as the main writer of it has altered the facts a bit. Joe Byrne just laughs and tells me that the Police have taken the liberty of altering all of their facts, 'so blow em all to hell,' he yells and rides faster.

CHAPTER FIFTEEN

I Can Take No More

We head for our old haunts and hideouts and feel that we are safe as we have many sympathisers and friends except for one Aaron Sherritt, who Mrs Byrne, Joe's mother, gets a message to us that Aaron Sherritt had indeed, just the other night, led superintendent Hare and seven troopers to her house with the intention of trapping the Kelly Gang there. Well, Joe is now furious and says that Aaron Sherritt, the scum who is keen on his sister, is now a dead man. I can see no way of stopping Joe when he is in this mood.

Meanwhile Maggie tells us that the Victorian Government is now fearful, that I Ned Kelly, was going to declare "Kelly Country" as an independent republic and me sympathisers were arming themselves ready for a revolution.

It is now mid-February eighteen seventy nine and still no letter of mine is printed. I can take no more and the thought of a revolution is really in my mind. If only they would let me Ma go, these thoughts would not be there. Maggie informs us now that Superintendent Hare and several troopers are camped around Mrs Byrnes house and that she has seen signs of them. She also tells me that a superintendent O'Connor has arrived from Queensland with six black troopers as we thought they had done previously but really have only just headed to the Kelly Country to try to track us down. Little does they know about me friend Jimmy and his group who have placed a curse on them. After another couple of weeks, Maggie brings news that Mrs Byrne has spotted the traps around her house and with them was Aaron Sherritt. Mrs Byrne has called off the engagement of her daughter Catherine to Sherritt. Maggie also tells us that the trackers from Queensland are having a tough time with the cold and wet of the high country and one of them, Corporal Sambo has died of pneumonia near Benalla.

Around this time, "Jimmy, finds his way to our camp and comes in peacefully by himself. I invites him to sit down and have a coffee and we talk. Jimmy tells me I will have no trouble with the trackers from Queensland as the local aboriginals of this area have put a curse on them. And this Sambo died from that curse. I thank Jimmy and give him a five pound note.

Maggie still brings us supplies on a regular basis and she tells me that the money I had passed on to appoint a good solicitor for the sympathisers who have been locked up for several weeks must have worked because they have all been discharged and Wild Wright sends his regards.

She tells me that the traps still camp around their hut every night waiting for me or Dan to show up. Maggie says that each night they let the dogs off their leads to put fear into the traps, who try poisoning the dogs, but me sisters put muzzles on the dogs.

Whenever me sisters get within ear shot of the traps, the traps they yells out they are going to shoot Dan and me on sight.

I asks Maggie if any of the traps have offended her or me sisters. She says no and I tells her to warn the traps that I will shoot them if they do. I feared not the trackers or the traps up here in the cold and deep snow.

I had more time now to write me letters, but I felt that I was truly wasting my time of nothing of what I had so far written had been properly published.

It was on a typically cold day, sitting on one of our never ending fires, when Joe Byrne said casually to me that he thought we were all dead men and I was wasting me time writing all that stuff. I stood up and threw all me letters into the fire and said "you're right mate". I then asked him to help me draw up some sketches of armour clothing that I had planned for us to wear as defence against the traps new rifles. Joe Byrne was a great help and it gave us all something to think about over those cold winter months.

Me Brother Dan filled in most of his day by singing or practicing his shooting. He was still daydreaming about going to South Africa and now Steve Hart was also keen on getting away although he was keener on going to America. Tom Lloyd pays us a visit for a few days and as sure as Irish is green, the sun comes up with his visit. An omen says he as he gives me a bundle of newspapers in which we have made the news, mostly on the front page. The Melbourne Age compares me with Premier Berry saying that I was probably more popular than he. It goes on to say that I probably had two thousand active sympathisers and it says I was a better bushman, a better rider, a better shot and a better leader than any of Berry's Police Force. Many of the newspapers had songs or poems about me or The Kelly Gang. One poem I remember clearly, it was sent in by the boy I saved from drowning. Dick Shelton it was but he's a man now and he wrote,

'Good on you Ned Kelly

We who know the real Ned

Say he's got fire in his belly

And sure has brains in his head

I thank you Ned for my life

Drowned I would have but for you

Now I'm married, two kids and a wife

So I say you Ned are one of a few.

We who know, understand your plight

All of your family, specially your Mother

Were hounded by Police both day and night

I Dick Shelton admire and respect you like a brother.'

Well, to say the least, this brought a tear to my eye as I read it.

Even though I had given up writing any letters as means of protest against the dictatorship of the government, I still thinks about me Jerilderie letter and how I challenge the authority of not only the Victorian and Australian governments, but of the authority of the English dictators, whose influence on Australia's government is still obvious. A rebellion had been accomplished against the English successfully in America, and Ireland are always yearning to be free of the English yolk. Even now, South Africa is on the brink of a war against the English oppressors so a dream of me leading a revolution to make Australia a republic is a possible thing.

A few days after Tom's visit Wild Wright arrives with the news that we have in fact over two thousand sympathisers ready to fight for what I believe is the right thing for the people. Wild Wright also, on behalf of the families of all the sympathisers who had been locked up during harvest time, thanks us, The Kelly Gang, for the monies that help the families get through these hard times.

The weather now seems to have broken and the snow thaws, so we leave the high country and go back to our own territory. We have no trouble evading the Police for many weeks and Maggie continues to bring us supplies and news of Police movements and who is informing on us to the Police. Patrick Quinn is dobbing on us she says, and Aaron Sherritt, who is now married, is on the Police payroll and receives seven shillings a day from them. She tells me that four Policemen are now living in the house with Sherritt as protectors. "He will keep" says Joe Byrne about Sherritt, 'but not for long,' he adds.

In March we The Kelly Gang decided to go to the Moyhu races as me sisters Maggie and Kate have entered the ladies hack race. We split up and stay near our horses ready to make a run for it if the traps see us. They don't and Wild Wright's fiancé Bridget Lloyd wins the ladies hack race from Maggie with Kate third. We had a good time, especially Dan that day.

By mid-March eighteen eighty we had started to pinch plough discs from some of the right pastoralists to make armours out of them for all The Kelly Gang to wear so the traps could not shoot us if a shootout did come. One of our sympathisers James Wallace travelled around in his buggy offering to buy these plough discs for us. When we had a good supply we built a big fire and got these plough discs red hot then laid them across green logs and hammered em into shape. Then we riveted the pieces together to make our armour. They were very heavy and we fired upon them to test whether or not the bullets would penetrate them but they did not, so I felt we were ready for anything the traps could try to shoot us with.

Maggie tells us, on one of her visits in April eighteen eighty that Constable Fitzpatrick had been sacked by the Police force for being a liar and a drunkard and for not doing his duty. 'So,' I says to Maggie, 'the traps, whose only evidence in court that they had, was from Fitzpatrick and they locks our Ma up on his word, and now they sack him and call him a liar. Surely they must let Ma out of goal now.' But no, me Ma stays in pentridge because of that liar Fitzpatrick.

I am now sick of the whole bleeding thing from start to now, and I says to Joe Byrne that we must do something about Sherritt because he is a paid informer and his continually informing to the traps is making it too difficult for us and Maggie says that he is watching her and telling the traps of her movements. I very firmly tell Joe that if me sister comes to harm because of Aaron Sherritt then you

Joe Byrne won't be dealing with your old school chum, I will. Joe says that this day June the twenty sixth eighteen eighty is Sherritt's last on this earth. Then he leaves to go, but Dan says 'I'm for helping you Joe.' Joe Byrne nods to me little brother then they go off.

The very next day Dan gives me a full report of what happened that night. Dan tells me that on the way to Sherritt's place they happened to bump into one of his neighbours, a Mr Anton Wicks, and Joe gets an idea, so he points his revolver at Wicks and duly handcuffs him with the cuffs he had taken from the Jerilderie police station. Joe tells him that we are part of the Kelly gang and if he does not do exactly as told then he would have to use this here pistol. This Dan tells me does the trick and after telling Wicks the plan, the three of em approach Sherritt's house, which they know has four traps inside guarding the informer that Joe is going to shoot. As told, and under two pistols the frightened Wicks knocks on the door and he calls out to tell Sherritt that it is Mr Wicks here and that he was a bit drunk and has lost his way.

Joe gives Dan his pistol and readies his shotgun with both barrels loaded. Dan goes on to tell me that it worked and Aaron Sherritt comes to the door and starts giving direction to Mr Wicks, who when he sees Joe come out from behind the tank, steps back and Joe Byrne shoots Sherritt twice, once in neck then again in the chest. Joe then yells 'you Aaron Sherritt will never DOB on us again you mongrel.'

Dan goes on to tell me that they then were expecting the four police to retaliate and were ready for a shootout, but all they heard was a women's scream and some footsteps inside the small house, so Dan and Joe look through the still open door to see the frightened police cowering in a corner, so me brother takes a shot at em, which frightens em even more and they rushes into a bedroom, so Joe fires towards em and they dive under the bed. 'Come out and fight, and stop hiding like bleeding cowards.' he yells at the four police, who are paid a good wage and under orders to protect the now dead informer Aaron Sherritt. 'Does they come out and fight you then?' I asks Dan, who shakes his head and tells me that Belle, or Mrs Sherritt, now a widow also dives under the bed which stops any more shooting at the scared traps as they might hit Belle.

Then says Dan we takes the cuffs off Mr Wicks and thanks him for his cooperation and tells him to go home. 'I'm very glad to be on your side,' says Wicks as he heads for home. 'Then,' says Dan, 'Joe and I comes back, to report to our leader, which is you Ned Kelly, me very Brother.'

CHAPTER SIXTEEN

Me Final Plan

I had been thinking a lot lately, especially since me brother had told me that he wants to start a new life and I had just about had enough, so me next plan was to bring the traps to us with a little surprise for em on the way. I tells Dan, Steve, and Joe of me plan, and how I reckoned it was time to have it out with Superintendent Hare and his men.

Our money was running a bit low, and I wanted to keep enough aside for any, or all of us who may get the opportunity to get away after this next decisive action I planned to force the traps into.

The main part of me plan was to let Hare know where we, "The Kelly Gang" were, and the first stage had been started with the extermination of Sherritt. This I knew would bring the traps running. But to where? Where is the best and most advantageous place to us for this to take place? Where would it be the easiest for all our 'Sympathisers' to gather and have this showdown, this probable start of the revolution by the oppressed and persecuted? To me the answer was clear, "Glenrowan."

So we loads our pack horses with all our weapons and ammunition and our completed and tested bullet proof armour, and for the surprise I had for em before they get to us we also loads a big drum of gunpowder, some fuses, plus some signal rockets. We arrive at Glenrowan to be met by some of the organizers of our sympathisers, and we hold a meeting and I tells em of me plan and direct them as to how they can best do their part. Steve Hart, who has had some experience with gunpowder joins me, and we leaves Dan and Joe at the Glenrowan Inn and we takes this very gunpowder and fuses plus two crowbars to a spot just north of town.

I looks at the lay of the land and picks a place where the railway tracks which I plan to use in me surprise for the trainload of traps will be coming along. Oh yes, I am confident that they will come because I had made sure a few informers were in the "know" about us being in Glenrowan supposedly celebrating the extermination of Aaron bleeding Sherritt. Firstly Steve using the crowbars, shifts and digs up part of these railway tracks, then we sets the drum of explosives to go off when the train leaves the tracks. Yes it is a good spot I ponders as I look at our work.

There is a nice curve and the land is lower on both sides so the train should roll over then be blown up. 'Nice work,' I tells Steve Hart and we ride the short distance back to the "Inn."

It is about three in the morning when we gets to where me brother and Joe Byrne are waiting. After telling them how we had set the surprise, we goes into the Glenrowan Inn where Mrs Anne Jones welcomes us, shows us a back room we can use, then cooks us a meal, after which we rests in this back room with one of us always awake, on guard.

I am up again at daylight and takes Joe with me and we arrests a few people. Firstly we gets the station master, who I instruct to turn off all the signal lights on the railway, and there was a few line worker nearby so in they come, and we locks em all in the front room of the Inn. I tells em that we are "The Kelly Gang," and if any one of you try to alarm the traps then I will have to shoot all of you, but if you behave then there is a good time to be had.

So I pays Anne Jones for drinks for everyone and encourage them to have a party on the Kelly Gang. I tells Steve Hart and Joe Byrne to keep an eye on this front room of prisoners and to arrest any more that come in, but to be sure and buy em all drinks and keep the party going as I wants the word to get to Superintendent Hare that we are here for the taking.

Little does Hare know of me plans, and even if they somehow get past me surprise on the railway tracks, he'll sure get a shock when we front em dressed in our bullet proof armour.

So Dan and I goes into the back room to lay out these armours so we can quickly put em on when the traps arrive. Me brother is very quiet as we now start to load our weapons which total, twenty six pistols, fourteen rifles, two shotguns and several thousand rounds of ammunition. 'What's up?' I asks Dan who stops loading and comes closer to me and looks me right in the eye, 'I did want to see me Ma one more time Ned,' he blurts out.

I did not know what to say to me brother, who, like me, had to grow up before he was really ready to be a man. I puts down me rifle and I says that we have come a long way in a short time and this is our showdown. 'This is our chance to show the traps for once and all.'

Dan smiles and tells me 'You know I love you me big brother, and I have done all and everything for you, and I'm now ready to die for you Ned, yes die, because we haven't got a hope in hell of beating em all. Sure we might blow up the train, but then a thousand of em will come and there can only be one end to it me brother.' I am stopped in me tracks now, for Dan is probably right. I Tells Dan again of me promise to our Ma, how I would let no harm come to him. 'Dan,' I says, 'if things go wrong you must obey me. Do you promise me this me brother?'

Up stands Dan and for a moment I thought he might challenge me, but he nods and says 'yes Ned I will obey you, but what if your plan goes wrong?' So I tells him that Joe Byrne and I have agreed that if the traps get the better of us, then you and Steve have to escape via the back way. Your horses will be waiting and Tom Lloyd is in on this plan and has arranged a place for you to go. 'I won't leave you Ned,' yells Dan, but I stops him and tells him that he has promised to obey me. 'But where will I go?' he asks. I tells him to go where his mind tells him to go.

Dan says, 'but I'm fighting with you.' I nods to him and tells him that is what I expect, but he must stop and go when I say. We now talk about old times for a while, and remember the good times. All goes quiet as we both know that our lives will almost certainly go down different paths. Then I gets out me knife and carefully I cuts a tiny square off the corner of me green sash that Mr Shelton gave to me. I gives this little piece of sash to me brother and I tells him that if we're separated, or I'm caught, he is to get this to me so I will know for sure that he is safe. Dan is a bit upset, but he tucks the piece of me sash away.

Then he says that every time he sings or hears the song "The Wild Colonial Boy" he will think of me. It is now very emotional for me as we both realize that whichever way the upcoming battle goes we will be separated, perhaps forever. I gathers myself together and gripping me young Brothers shoulder, I says, 'whenever I hears me favourite song "Danny Boy," it's you I'll be thinking about.'

I quietly tells him, 'Go now and tell Steve himself about our plan then.'

THE SPIRIT OF NED

I finish loading the rest of the weapons and I make sure our bullet proof armours are laid out ready for us to quickly put on when the traps arrive. I am sure they will come here to Glenrowan. The temptation will be too much for Hare and Steele and their trigger happy men to let go by.

They will be almost counting the eight thousand pounds reward money that they have openly bragged they were after.

I am finished here so, I make me way into the main front room where the party is in full swing. There must be fifty or more prisoners and sympathisers in there by now and I put more money on the bar and tell em all to drink up.

There are two Inns at Glenrowan, the other one being owned by Paddy McDonnell, and sure enough, not one to miss out on what's going on, Paddy has brought his family over the road to Anne Jones's place and he beckons me over and asks 'what is going on Ned?' I am not real sure that I can trust him or his wife who is well known to unable to keep a secret, so I tells Paddy that we are just having a shindig. I orders and pays for drinks for him and his family. As I start to leave, Paddy says to me 'we are with you Ned.'

Then I talks to the McAuliffe brothers, and many more who I knows to be on our side. One of the Lloyds finds his way over to me and says that he has over eighty men armed and ready to come at my call. I tells him that if I decides that I does need him I will let go a signal rocket.

He nods, then tells me he has arranged for a German couple a few miles away to take in Dan and Steve, if it comes to that, and that he has their horses ready out the back of Paddy's place. He starts to go back to his men then I calls him back and asks him, if all goes wrong would he visit me mother and tell her I loves her, and tell her if Dan is safe.

He opens the door to go just as two fit looking young men enter, so I points me pistol at em and tells em they are now prisoners of "The Kelly Gang," then I buys em a drink and asks em where they are from. They tell me that they are from not far away and they are fruit pickers. 'Well me lads,' I tells em, straight, 'you must now stay in this here room, cause if you try to leave then the population of your town will be two less. Do you understand?' They both agree, and at me invitation they order a jug of Anne Jones special homemade brew, and they head for a table with the obvious plan of getting drunk. On their table I leaves enough money for their drinks, and more.

Still more people that I know come in, and I tells em all that all the drinks are on me. Then I notices Dan and Steve talking together so I makes me way over, amid people talking to me and thanking me for the drinks, and finally I gets to me brother and his best friend.

I pulls out me money bag and hands em both a hundred pounds each and tells em that it's for getting away money. Steve Hart shakes me hand, 'Thank you Ned, Dan has told me, and I'm for fighting with you,' he says. 'Until I tells you both to go, then you will go,' I says.

CHAPTER SEVENTEEN

'*Shindig at Glenrowan*'

By now most of the district has heard of the "Kelly Gang Shindig" and either come to join in, or some come just for a look. Inside the main room of Anne's Inn, there are about a dozen armed sympathisers, most of them being former members of 'The Greta Mob', and they help keep an eye on all in the room, making sure that no one leaves.

Old Martin Cherry wanders in and tells me to arrest him and let him join the famous 'shindig'. I laughs and gets him a good seat, and I notice he is carrying his famous accordion, or "Squeeze Box," as he calls it. 'Mind if I plays a bit of music to get this place hopping,' the old but happy man asks. I tells him it's a bleedin good idea, and calls for quiet and introduces him to the merry crowd, and sure enough Mr Cherry plays his heart out and the hands are clapping and the feet are tapping everywhere.

I then decides to go outside for a breather and just then a buggy driven by the local schoolmaster Mr Thomas Curnow pulls up at the front of the Inn. I makes me way through the crowd and tells Thomas Curnow that I'm Ned Kelly, and he introduces his wife Isobel his baby, and his brother in law. He says that his wife has been tending to Anne Jones who has been sick lately.

I says 'Well you're good wife may do that, and the rest of you must stay in the Inn and do as I say, then no harm will become you.'

After Mrs Curnow has tended to Anne, I gets Steve Hart to escort her and her baby back to the Curnow's house, and I tells him to stay with them until I sends for him. I then go back inside to see that Dan has cleared some of the furniture away to make a dance floor, and he is soon up jigging around. Someone mentions that Thomas Curnow is a good dancer, so Dan gets him up and they and a few others dance away to Martin Cherry's music.

Food, and plenty of it is now laid out on a couple of tables, and I pays Anne Jones for it. After most of us have eaten, and the room is fairly quiet an old man who no one has taken much notice of makes his way to the middle of this very room, then looks across at me and says, "with your permission Mr Kelly,' he asks to which I duly nod. 'I have written a poem just now and I wish to recite it.' In a good Irish voice he takes the floor, and we all listen,

> *'Tis the day the Kelly Gang came down.*
> *From their hideout in the hills they came,*
> *To give a shindig here in Glenrowan,*
> *And I think I'll join in, if it's all the same.*
> *For it's on the Kelly's side that I am,*
> *Cause I know the true story,*
> *Of how they were hounded to a man,*
> *By those traps who were chasing glory.*
> *So thank you Ned Dan, Steve and Joe*
> *For this shindig that we sure enjoy.*
> *And this story will spread everywhere we go,*
> *Like the time when you Ned did save that boy.*
> *We who know you will stand by you till the end.*
> *Yes, Ned Kelly you are a leader of men,*
> *And we'll do you're bidding, just you say when.*
> *Thanks for the party Ned, I just had to attend.'*

The elderly gentleman takes off his hat and bows to the applauding crowd, then makes his way back to his seat in a corner. I asks Anne Jones if she knows who this man is and she tells me he has only been around Glenrowan a few days. I decides to go and talk to this man of poetry. As I get near to him I see that he is a big man, and I sort of feel like I could be looking at me very self. 'Hello to ye Ned,' he says. I takes his outstretched hand and shake it.

THE SPIRIT OF NED

He tells me his name is Quin, Robert Quin. So I then sits down and when I enquire as to whether we are related as me grandfather's name was Quinn, he just says 'could be that we are kinfolk.' I am not sure what to say to Robert Quin, but he breaks the silence by asking me if me mother Ellen ever spoke of a Mr Thomas Quin, so I tells him that she had said a Thomas Quinn used to visit them in Ireland. I says, 'from Ballina, I think she said he was.' We are interrupted by Dan who comes to me and says some of the people wants to see the Kelly brothers do a bit of trick riding. I tries to introduce Dan to Robert, but me brother is now dragging me to get our horses.

With the sympathisers guarding the Inn, Dan and meself put on a show doing tricks and riding bare back on our horses for about an hour we do this. Dan stole the show with his trick of picking a handkerchief off the ground with his teeth again. Then me Brother does the hardest trick we have ever tried. Dan stands on one foot on the back of his horse at full gallop. When we have finished one of our friends takes our horses and I reminds him to have Dan and Steve's horses ready out the back.

We goes back inside and I can't find this Robert Quin so I sits back and watch the shindig continue. After few minutes I am surprised when David Mortimer, who is the Brother in law of Thomas Curnow, brings out a fiddle and really livens things up, so much so that Dan Asks Thomas Curnow to dance with him again but Dan is taken aback when the schoolmaster refuses.

Joe Byrne, who has probably had too much whiskey, runs over and points his pistol at Curnow and says, 'if you value your life Curnow, then you will not refuse Dan Kelly a dance.' They are joined by many others, and as soon as the dance ends and there is almost silence in this big parlour.

Then a voice as clear as crystal spreads its way from thirteen year old Jack Jones, the son of Anne, to right throughout the room. Everyone stops and listens to this wonderful singer, whose voice has not yet broken and is almost like a soprano.

This very voice is then joined by another sweeter, more mellow but softer voice, and I look to the corner and it young Jacks Sister Jane who has joined him, and they perform a song they must have learned at school. When they finished, and the applause finally stops the young Brother and Sister walk slowly over to me and Jack Jones says to me, 'Mr Kelly sir, I have been practising a ballad which could be about your very self, and I would like to sing it to you if it pleases you sir.' I say that I am pleased, so he sings to me, then the fiddle player starts to accompany him and it is quite eerie as they reach the high notes.

When he stops, and the crowd stops cheering, Joe jumps up onto the bar and says to them, 'you people who on behalf of The Kelly Gang I thank for sharing this time with us, I ask you to remember this day. Remember how you were the guests of Ned Kelly who has been wrongly done by, whose mother has been wrongly locked away. But mostly remember that Ned Kelly is not a bad fellow.' I am touched by all this, but say nothing.

Then blow me over with a feather Anne Jones brings her daughter with her and they sing again this ballad that Jack had sung. As they reach the chorus everyone joins in,

> "FAREWELL TO MY HOME IN GRETA,
> MY LOVED ONES FARE THEE WELL,
> IT BREAKS MY HEART TO LEAVE
> BUT HERE I MUST NOT DWELL."

So the good times go on.

CHAPTER EIGHTEEN

Thomas Curnow

We have been here for over a day and a half, and I am starting to wonder that the traps might not take me bait and come here to Glenrowan after all. Dan, who is now only drinking tea or water, tells me that he does not think they will come, but I say that we will stay longer yet. It is the afternoon of the twenty seventh of June in the year eighteen eighty and I notice that the shindig is starting to slow down. Old Martin Cherry is quiet, the two young fruit pickers are still drinking homemade wine, and are looking quite drunk. Mrs Jones and her children have gone for a rest.

It is in this Quiet period that the schoolmaster, Thomas Curnow comes over to me and tells me that I seem to have forgotten that Constable Bracken is still in his hut at the police quarters. I gets s bit suspicious as he seems to have come to help me, but I decides to go to get Bracken and bring him back to the Inn.

I starts off but Curnow stops me and says it would be a good idea if I was to take someone who Constable Bracken knows. 'Let's go then,' I says, but Curnow tells me that his brother in law David Mortimer is better known to the Policeman, so I takes Mortimer and when we reaches the police quarters I gets him to call out the Constable who is a fair while coming out. 'He has been ill,' says Mortimer.

Then finally out comes Bracken, and is caught by surprise and raises his hands when he sees me pistol aimed at him. 'You can't be here Ned Kelly. It's the laughing stock of the whole force that I will be now,' he cries. 'It's not the laughing you has to think about, but the lead in this here pistol,' I tells him. I gets him to tell his wife that he will be down at the Inn for a while, and he is to give me all his weapons and ammunition.

He brings out a revolver and a shotgun but not many bullets, and he says there are no more. 'Stop lying like a copper Bracken and get me all the ammunition if you don't want your wife to be a widow,' and this changes his attitude and he produces two boxes of bullets for each gun. So the Glenrowan Inn has another "prisoner" whom I buys a drink for, and to my surprise Bracken raises his glass and drinks to me health. I raise me glass and return the toast, then he says that I must not repeat what he is going to say, and if I does he will deny having ever said it.

Quietly I sit and listen as this Constable tells me that most of the policemen feel that us Kelly's have been hard done by, and he has heard some of the senior officers brag in the past, even before Stringybark Creek, that they were going to shoot the Kelly's down on sight, and even "back shoot you." I raises me glass to him and tells him that if the Victorian police force had more like him and less like Hare, Steele and Fitzpatrick then we would not be here ready to take some revenge today.

Bracken nods and tells me that Fitzpatrick is a hated man in the force, and has been sacked and branded a liar and a coward. 'This does not free me mother from gaol,' I says. He says he and many good policemen are sorry.

Thomas Curnow comes over to me as I leave Bracken at the bar, and he asks me permission to take his wife and family home where they would be safer. I hesitate, and Curnow says that surely he has proven to be trustworthy as he has just reminded me about Constable Bracken. I makes me first big mistake in me plan and gets Joe Byrne to escort him and his family to his home, but I tells Joe to bring Curnow himself back here.

It's now just after midnight and it's too quiet so I says at the top of me voice, 'who will be the one to start a concert for The Kelly Gang?' Martin Cherry stagger's to the small stage and croons out the old song.

"Surrender now Jack Doolan,

You see there's three to one,

Surrender now Jack Doolan'

You daring highwayman.

Jack drew a pistol from his belt,

And shook it like a toy.

I'll fight not surrender,

Cried the wild colonial boy."

So I joins in and to me surprise, so does Joe Byrne, who seemed to have got back from the Curnow's pretty quickly. We all sing the verse with Martin Cherry a couple of times, then someone else says a poem, during which I says to Joe that he was not long in taking the Curnow family home, and I says to him, 'where is Mr bleedin Curnow anyway?'

Joe who starts to have another drink tells me that the schoolmaster was not feeling well and wanted to stay at his home. I shakes me head and tell Joe he better lay off the drink as the traps could be coming at any time. I truly thought that me old mate Joe was going to challenge me there and then, but he looks away, puts his drink down and says 'sure thing Ned, I'm a dead man anyway.' Dan is now sober and up singing and dancing and I looks at me nineteen year old brother, about to take on half the bleeding police force, and here he is, large as life itself, starting to sing our song for all Glenrowan to hear.

'Oh Danny boy, the pipes, the pipes are calling,' and I joins in as does the crowd, and when we finish Dan comes to me and we embrace like Brothers. Then I says that the Kelly Brothers will now take to the floor, and I asks the musicians to strike up then I asks Jane and Dan asks Anne Jones to accompany us to the dance floor.

We do dance, even though Dan is a good dancer I am the opposite. I seem to have grown another foot and it gets in the way. Anyway the crowd seems to like it and many get up and join in. After the dance is over the musicians keep the mood merry with good old Irish jigs and Anne Jones brings heaps of hot food and hot tea for all. I pays her more money, and then she sits near me and we eat together, I takes this chance to thank her for the hospitality she has shown us. 'But Ned, you have more than paid for it all, but I'll be telling you something Ned Kelly, I would not have missed this shindig for anything,' she says. Anne Jones the proprietor of this Glenrowan Inn goes on to tell me that she reckons that this party, and what is about to follow will go down in Australian history and folklore.

It is now that feel I must tell her what is really happening, or is likely to happen, after which I says to her that I think it is time to let everyone except constable Bracken go for their own safety. 'Including you Anne, and your children, because there may be bullets flying here soon.' She smiles at me then kisses me on the cheek and tells me she is not going anywhere, 'but thank you for telling me Ned, even though I did already know.'

'You Innkeepers know everything that's going on don't you Mrs Pretty Jones,' I tells her. This fine lady then stands up, looks me in the eye and quietly says, 'please dance with me one last time Ned Kelly.' We dance together for several minutes, and for the first time in me short life, me left foot behaves and I probably am dancing well. When the music stops this pretty lady does not break our embrace, but kisses me and says 'thank you Ned, I will never forget you.'

A little later I remembers Thomas Curnow and I gets Joe Byrne to go and check on the schoolmaster, and to go to the stationmasters house and tell Steve Hart to let the prisoners go and to come back here with you. I thinks that the walk in the cold air will do Joe good and maybe even sober him up, but I tells him 'don't be long Joe because I'm expecting the train load of traps at any time now.'

I walk around the room and again tell everyone that they are free to go, and when I gets to Martin Cherry, god bless him, I tells him it might be safer if he was to go home, he says to me, 'Home is where me next drink is Ned.'

Next to him the two young blokes that have been drinking nonstop for two days are asleep, or passed out from too much of the cheap wine they have been drinking for too long. It is not uncommon for people to die from drinking too much cheap wine. I gets Dan to give me a hand and we takes em into the back room where they will be safer, and they might sleep it off. One of em half opens his eyes and slurs out, 'Thass Ned Kelly ishsinit?' Then he passes out again. Dan and I just get back into the front room as Joe Byrne and Steve Hart come in. Joe is panting as he tells me that Curnow was not at home and his wife said she did not know where he went, but he was carrying a red lamp. 'Bleedin hell,' I yells. 'He's gone to warn the train.' Yes, I thinks, Thomas Curnow has outsmarted all of us.

CHAPTER NINETEEN

It's What We Are Here For

Dan says, 'listen'. Sure enough we all now hear the train and me mind takes over in a sort of calm way and I say to Dan, Steve, and Joe, 'Well, this is it then, this is what we are here for.' I tells em to come to the back room and we all put on our armours and trench coats. Me plan was to mount up and ride to the train crash, and or explosion area and finish off the traps there once and for all. But as we go back to the front room dressed in our armour one of our sympathisers runs in and tells me that Curnow did warn the train in time and they have disarmed the gunpowder booby trap and fixed the line and are now on the way here.

Also he says Constable Bracken was seen running from here to obviously tell the about twenty or thirty traps where "The Kelly Gang" is holed up. I looks around and sure enough Bracken is gone. He must have made his run while we were getting changed. 'Well then, a change of plans,' I says and decides that we will meet them here out the front of this very Inn, in our bullet proof armour. We all have either a rifle or a shotgun each, plus four or five revolvers stuck in our armour wherever we could fit them.

I orders anyone still left in the Inn to lay low so they are below bullet range, and I tell the sympathiser to go back to the place where the about eighty armed others are waiting for me instructions or me signal rocket to go off which would mean they are to come and join in the fight. But not everyone will leave, saying, 'we are with you Ned.'

Then we four "Kelly gang" members goes out to wait for the traps on the veranda. We feel confident dressed in our bullet proof armours, and we reckon the traps think that we are asleep and don't know they are coming. I had organized for Anne Jones to put out all lights and the fire so the traps would have trouble seeing us as I wanted surprise on our side. I orders the other three to stay in the shadows on "The Glenrowan Inn" veranda, while I moves to the end closest to where I can now just see a group moving slowly towards us.

They surely know we are here as they are heading straight at us, so I know for sure Constable Bracken, who I did respect, must have told em that we were here, but the confident way they were moving makes me think that they think we are asleep, so we do have surprise on our side. Me hopes of using this surprise, are raised when I now see superintendent Hare leading about four troopers and half a dozen or so fully armed native trackers.

Good, I thinks, Hare is striding straight at me and as he gets about forty yards from me I aims me rifle and in this bright moonlight I knows I won't miss such a big target as this six foot three inch trap, but just as I am starting to squeeze the trigger on me trusty rifle to shoot this very man who for two years has been hounding all me families including me sisters, telling em how he was going to shoot us on sight like dogs, one of the other traps near Hare, spies me and shouts a warning that saves the life of his Superintendent.

I still fires but Hare has moved to bring his gun to bear, and me bullet hits him in his hand and he drops his gun and yells, 'I am hit.' Dan, Steve and Joe now start to open fire on the traps as they dive for cover. Hare who is well hidden, calls out 'surrender in the name of the Queen.' Dan calls back in his loudest voice, 'surrender be buggered.' We all fire at will at the traps and now Joe Byrne yells loudly to em 'come on you Bastards. You can't do us any harm.'

All goes quiet for a moment then I calls for em to surrender to us, "The Kelly Gang." Then I walks towards em and I am now not so clear headed as me years of anger and frustration get the better of me, and I make meself an easy target. As I walks at em I yell and shoot like a wild mantis. Then I feels a bullet smash into me right foot but I won't let meself fall or I'm a goner. The traps are firing madly too except for Hare who I see making a run for it back towards the train station.

Another bullet smashes into me left arm and it feels like a piece of dangling meat, so I walks back into the shadows. Joe Byrne then yells that he has been hit, he copped a bullet in his right leg, down in the calf area. I can now see another group of traps heading our way and as soon as they are in range I open fire. Most of the traps are now shooting directly into the Inn, but all this time we had been on the veranda or near its why have they been firing into the building?

I am shocked to hear Anne Jones Scream out that young Jack Jones has been badly hit. Then she says that she has been shot and so has her daughter. I now notice the top of me right thumb is missing in action but I don't feel much pain, though I am losing a lot of blood and am starting to feel dizzy. Should I call for reinfor'cements. I cannot think clearly, and I'm almost passing out, so I missed the chance of winning the battle, by not calling in the waiting sympathisers. I Now I reckon that we have not much hope as things have gone against us. I shakes me head to try to think clearly, and I realize that now is the time to get Dan and Steve away.

CHAPTER TWENTY

Goodbye Me Brother

Joe Byrne and I are together and Dan and Steve are too far away for me to talk to em and I reckon I am near done for, so I tells Joe to tell Dan and Steve that I orders em to go now as planned, and I asks him to tell Dan that I says 'goodbye me brother.'

I force meself to front the now probably thirty traps, and I find I can't lift me weapons high enough but I just keep firing at em the best I can, but even though its moonlight I don't think they can properly see me, although bullets are smacking into me armour by the dozen. I must have kept em busy so Dan and Steve could get away, but somehow I find I am now behind the police line and I can see them either looking for me or firing wildly at the "Inn." 'Not finished with em yet,' I says to me very self, but I feel real dizzy now, and I must have gone for a trip to the land of nod, for when I opens me eyes next the sun is near ready to come up and there is thick fog all around.

I gets up again and find me way back to the Inn. Me thoughts were wandering and I seemed to be dreaming because when I does make it to the Inn, there is Joe still firing away, and I knew he had not seen me coming, so I yells to him, and when he now sees me he says 'bleeding hell Ned, you must be charmed. 'You have been through the traps line and back again, and I thought you were a goner.' I tell Joe that I am proud of him and that I knew he would fight to the end, then I gets him to reload all me weapons, then I snaps out of me dream like feeling and asks him if Dan and Steve got away. Joe Byrne nods and points to the back of the Inn and tells me that they left the back way, and they left their armours in the back room near the two young blokes who look like they have drunk themselves to bleeding death.

There are still sympathisers laying low, and as I look around I can't see Anne Jones so I ask Joe if the Jones got out alright. 'Not really,' Joe says,' 'they were all shot by the traps, and I think young Jack is a goner.' I looks to where old Martin Cherry had been when I last seen him, and he was laying as though he was dead.

It was over, I am not going to signal the group of sympathisers who were armed and ready to mount their horses and come to our aid. I did not want these good men to have any trouble like we have been through, so I says to Joe Byrne, 'Well mate it's now or never, will you join me as I am going this time to finish it all one way or the other.'

Joe tells me that he is with me to the end. 'But, I'm for one last drink Ned,' and he goes to the bar of this very Glenrowan Inn and pours himself a whiskey, looks at me for what is to be the last time cause as he raises his drink and says, 'to the brave Kelly Gang,' a bullet from the traps hits him under the armour and me best friend Joe Byrne falls down dead. "The Kelly Gang" is no more.

Then I mumble a last goodbye to me best mate Joe Byrne, but I know that me Brother Dan, and his best mate Steve Hart are away to live on, thank God.

I am now digging deep into my reserves of what strength I have left, then as I look at the body of Joe, and think how the traps have, by firing into the Inn, while we were outside, they have murdered young Jack Jones and Martin Cherry. Thinking like this gets me temper up and I check me weapons, then I grabs Joe Byrnes pistol as well and I makes sure me armour is on properly and I am ready. Me only regret is I would have liked to have said 'Goodbye Me Brother,' to Dan. I have worked meself into a fit of madness now, and I am ready, and I go to give em all I have got.

CHAPTER TWENTY ONE

Game or Mad?

As I head towards what must surely be me end, I wonders if I am maybe mad to take on so many traps by meself. I have never thought of me, Ned Kelly as being game, though I have never backed or bowed down to those who have hounded me and me family. So game or not, I am surely mad right now. Mad with temper. Then suddenly a calm comes over me. This is the same calm that I felt when I was in trouble in the deep swirling creek when I saved young Dick Shelton from drowning. I now fear nothing as I am getting close to the traps who are still shooting wildly at the Glenrowan Inn. I start shooting at the nearest of em who are surprised that I am there.

Most of me shots fall short of them, but I can see that they are scared, and some even run for their lives as I appear out of the trees with fog around me, the full moon starting to fade and the sun just showing its head, I must have looked like a monster coming at em. But not all of the traps are frozen with fear or trepidation, and I feel dozens of bullets hit me armour and helmet and I wishes that I had not taken me skullcap from under me helmet cause the bullets banging against me helmet is making me bleed a lot. I hears one trap call out that he has shot me and there is blood pouring out of me helmet.

I yells at him, 'shot me have you, you mongrel,' as I throw down me empty rifle and draws one of me many revolvers I have tucked in me armour. I shoot at him and either I hit him or went close cause he disappeared mighty quickly. I hears another voice yell, 'it's a Bunyip and we can't kill it.' The bullets hitting me increase as all the traps now seem to have come to join in. The slugs make a ringing noise just like the old church bell at Beechworth, and I makes even more ringing noises as I taps me helmet with the butt of me revolver which taunts em more. The firing now reaches a crescendo and I shouts to em, 'FIRE AWAY YOU BUGGERS.' Now hundreds of pieces of lead bounce off me armour and it is a miracle that not one of these bullets finds its way through the slit in me helmet.

I fire at any body that presents itself to me, and this usually makes em duck for cover. Another revolver is empty so I pulls out the Webley pistol that Joe had taken from Lonigan at Stringy Bark Creek. As I looks for a target, I hears a voice I know and I look and there is Sergeant rotten Steele who fires at me and shoots Joe's pistol fair out of me hand. So I pulls out another and I walks into the open and I shouts to Steele, 'come on you murderer Steele, you can't hurt me.'

I feels about a half a dozen slugs bounce off me back, so I turn to see a Constable Dowset standing only a couple of yards from me and he shouts for all of Glenrowan to hear, 'this must be the very Devil, I cannot hurt the monster.' Then he draws another revolver and fires away at me head, and as the smoke from his gun clears he can't believe that I am still alive and standing. 'Throw up your hands,' he says.

'Not while I have any shots left in this,' I say to him as I points me pistol at him and as I fire he ducks and runs like a rabbit.

I somehow sense Steele in coming at me so I turns and fires at him but I can't hold me arm up high enough and so I miss, but before I can try to lift me arm again Steele dives behind a big log. The mongrel then bobs up this time with a shotgun and he shoots both barrels into unprotected legs. I am near done for, but I keeps firing even though Steele is again hiding behind the log. He must have reloaded his shotgun because here he is again aiming at me legs, and here I am me pistol empty, just able to stand and sure enough he fires both barrels into me legs again. I topples over and lands on me face.

'Enough, I am done,' I yells but again I feels bullets from a shotgun rip into legs and then they are onto me. Steele or one of em rip me helmet off, 'by the heavens its Ned himself,' someone cries. By now they have rolled me over and now, though I am barely conscious, and can only just see, I knows it is Steele. He has already fired upon women and kids, and I knows he won't hesitate to now shoot me.

He gives an awful smile and slowly brings his pistol to bear at me head and I know now that I'm a dead man. In what I reckon are me last moments on this very earth, I sees me Ma's face before me eyes, and I think's surely Ma you know that I have kept me word and Dan is away. It seems like an eternity those last few seconds waiting for Steele to pull the trigger.

Then as if struck by lightning, Steele is physically knocked away, and I hears the voice of Constable Bracken. 'I'll shoot anyone that tries to shoot Ned.' I look with welcome disbelief and see Bracken point his cocked shotgun at Steele, then he says to the coward Steele, 'do not try to shoot him, he never done me any harm.'

Constable Dowset, who god bless him must also have been upset with Steele actions, pushes his Sergeant away and says loudly, 'take him alive.' Constable Bracken still menaces Steele with his shotgun and says to the by now about twenty or thirty traps and onlookers in a loud threatening voice, 'I AM GOING TO TAKE HIS PART.'

CHAPTER TWENTY TWO

They Have Me

As I start to drift into unconsciousness I hear Bracken give orders to other traps. I faintly hears him tell someone to go to the other side of the Inn and ask the officers to stop firing as the bullets are going straight through the timber walls and some are reaching to where the police are stationed on this side. I drifts in and out of consciousness and each time I wake up I see more and more traps and reporters and I suppose onlookers, wanting to get a look at me.

Dr Nicholson arrives and he takes over, and makes all the people stand back as he tends to me wounds. 'I can do no more for this man here,' the Doctor tells Constable Bracken. Steele must have left, not happy with his treatment from Constable's Bracken and Dowsett, and I am pleased to have seen the last of the mongrel.

The good doctor steps away so I may not be able to hear him, but I does hear him, and he tells Bracken that I have too many bullets in me, and I have lost too much blood, and any ordinary man would already be dead. I drift off again and the next thing I know I am being walked or sort of dragged. Then I am in the train station office, and on a stretcher and all me armour and clothes are gone and I am covered in a blanket.

Then I notice me sash is missing and I reckon some sod has pinched it, so I asks Doctor Nicholson to get it please. A few moments pass then Bracken comes in with me sash and tells me that Steele had it on his person. 'So I took it off him with perhaps a little force,' he tells me. I thanks Bracken, and as I told him a couple of days ago I tells him again, that if all Policemen were like him, then this country would be better off. Doctor Nicholson nods to Bracken and points to the door and thinks I hear someone weighing me armour, and he exclaims loudly, 'ninety seven pounds.' Several newspapermen are trying to come in to this makeshift hospital, but again the good Doctor refuses to let em in.

This very Doctor is writing down a list of me injuries and is speaking them as he writes, 'Ned Kelly, aged about twenty five. Two black eyes, a torn cheek, a battered nose, abrasions all over his body, two bullet wounds in left arm, one bullet wound in right arm, twenty five other probable shotgun wounds, bullet to right foot, and;' I must have faded off and when I opens me eyes next another Doctor is also working on me.

This new to me man helping attend me wounds, upon seeing me open me eyes, says to me 'Welcome back Ned. We thought we may have lost you.' He goes on, 'I am Dr Hutchinson. How do you feel?' I tells this Doctor that I feel like I have been to Waterloo. Then I feel I am fading off, and I think I hears Doctor Hutchinson say to someone, that if we don't stabilise him we will lose him. When I next come back to almost life, there looking at me is Superintendent Sadleir.

He asks me if I could do with a brandy which he has in his hand ready. I figure that if I am going to die, then what it matters if I have a brandy, so I thanks him, drinks it down, and asks for another. The second drink I takes me time with, and being not too sure why this man that is the one in charge of destroying "The Kelly Gang" is here, and why one day sending near all the Victorian Police Force with orders to shoot me, then all of a sudden he calls me Ned, and brings me brandy?

I soon finds out by asking him just that. This Superintendent, in his best voice, as though he is on the bleeding stage and not here in this makeshift Hospital says 'Ned Kelly, on behalf of all the decent police officers in the Victorian force, I humbly apologize to you and your family.' I tells him I don't think there are too many good or decent men in the police force like you Superintendent. Then I says 'Now, please tell me why you're here really here Sir.' This man sure has a way with words, here he is, he's just been told I'm on the brink of me death and he goes on, 'you shall have every care and attention Ned.'

Then he comes to the part as to why he is really here. He asks me to send word to the others of me gang still in the Glenrowan Inn asking them to give themselves up. I then realize that they don't know that Dan and Steve have escaped, and poor Joe is dead.

He says, 'you can save lives Ned, if you can get them to surrender.' Dizzy now and barely conscious I somehow manage to mumble to Sadleir, 'I am sure none of them will ever surrender.' I am now drifting off as I hear Doctor Nicholson order everyone out except him and Doctor Hutchinson, but Sadleir says that Ned Kelly must be guarded at all times. The good Doctor loses his temper now and I hear him loudly say. 'You have tied this man up like a chook about to have its head cut off and you say he needs guarding. Well then guard him from outside this room. He is my patient so OUT, all of you.' This is not a man to mess with, so out them all go.

When I next open me eyes, I can tell by the light through the window that it is about mid-morning, and for a while I am not able to think or understand where I am. Then I hear the odd shot from the direction of the Inn so either there are still some sympathisers inside the place or the traps could be still firing from both sides and the bullets are going straight through the building and the traps on either side think it's someone from inside firing. Me mind starts to work a bit better now, and I realize where I am.

I asks Dr Nicholson if he can see what's going on out there and he tells me there more police coming all the time and they have completely surrounded the Inn and some look like recruits who want to be able to tell their grandchildren how they fired upon "The Kelly Gang." He says there are hundreds of civilians watching also. The shooting still goes on, but now there is another sound, which is getting louder by the minute.

People it is, and they are booing and jeering. Then I work out that the must be objecting to the Police, who are still firing wildly into the Glenrowan Inn. Again I drift away and next thing I know young Michael Reardon is carried into this makeshift hospital for treatment. He says hello to me and when he gets the chance sometimes when no one can hear, he tells me that me brother is safe. I thank him, and ask him what happened to him.

'Those murdering traps shot me,' he says. Michael then tells me that earlier when there had been a break in the firing, his mother said that we must get out, so she carried their baby, 'and with me and Dad leading our two sisters we step outside with me mother screaming to the traps not to shoot, and this Sergeant Steele yells, 'come this way or I will shoot you.'

Young Michael who is about seventeen, goes on to tell me, 'this murdering Steele opens fire at us and does not stop, and one shot grazed our baby's head, then me mother makes a run for the station but I turn back cause I thought I had no chance, then me Dad grabbed our two sisters just as Steele turns his attention to us as our mother had made it to the station, and the swine shoots me in the back.' Michael then tells that a crowd gathered round him as he lay on the ground in pain and unable to move, then he thought this Steele was going to shoot him again.

'Then' this brave lad tells me, 'Ned, the strangest thing happened. Another Policeman rushes at Steele and with his revolver aimed at this murdering Steele, he says that if he doesn't stop trying to murder innocent people then he would shoot him right here and now.' We are interrupted and they takes Michael Reardon to a different room.

Soon coming in to me room I sees a priest and I thinks I'm done for now, as he probably has come to read me last rites. 'Hello to you Ned, I am Father Gibney,' he tells me in a fine Irish voice.

CHAPTER TWENTY THREE

Am I Dead?

I try to keep awake but it is hard to do, but I does me best out of respect for this fine priest, who tells me he is from Western Australia and is on a fund raising mission in Albury. 'But the train has stopped here,' he says. 'God has sent me to you Ned Kelly.' I thank him for coming and request that he prepare me for death. Doctor Nicholson hears me make this request, and leaves me alone with Father Gibney.

I am told what to say, and I do so properly, and then he tells me I should now pray for forgiveness, after which I tells him I have done this many times. It is hard to be able to hear what father Gibney is saying to me because there are many more shots ringing out all the time, and I thinks it is a good thing Dan and Steve took off when they did. 'If it pleases you Ned, I will now hear your confession,' he says and after I give my confession he anoints me with holy oil, then he looks at me for a full minute, then says 'I do believe god has forgiven you my son.' I thank this fine priest. Then he is gone as if he has received a message.

The next time I awaken, there is me Sisters Maggie and Kate looking at me, but they are both crying openly. 'Cry not please,' I says to them, and they both rush to embrace me. 'I will give you two minutes alone,' says Doctor Nicholson, and as he moves to the passage I sees Wild Wright standing there in the doorway and I nods to him and he does the same back to me. Maggie sits close and I whispers that our brother is away and safe and so is Steve. 'But,' I says me voice choking, 'Joe copped it bad and is dead.'

Maggie quizzes me more and I tell her that Dan and Steve's armours are laid out next to the bodies of two young blokes that drank themselves to death, and they are in the back room. Me sisters both now hold me and tell me they are proud of me and I am not to die. They both say this to me many times. Maggie, dear Maggie, says between sobs, 'Ned, if you do die, we will remember you forever.'

Superintendent Sadleir now comes to the door but can't get past the big frame of Wild Wright, who tells him 'our two minutes are not up yet Mr Sadleir.' Well Sadlier storms off and does not come back for five minutes, during which, in between me drifting off we talk about old times, and I asks me sisters to tell Ma that I'm sorry. 'Also tell her that I kept me promise about Dan. They are then called to go and I manage to say I loves em and to tell Ma I loves her. Tears flow openly now, especially from Kate and then they are gone.

The loss of so much blood must have weakened me cause I now feel that the Doctors might be right, and the Good Father Gibney needed to give me the 'Last Rites'. As I lay on me mattress, I really don't know whether I am alive or dead. Everything is hazy, and I seem to be floating above me own body looking down, and I can see the two Doctors working on me and one of em is pumping me chest, but I can't feel anything. Then from a long way in the distance I hears this voice and I think it's me Dad calling me, 'Ned, wake up. Come on, wake up.'

I wants so much to go to me Dad, and he keeps calling me, 'Come on me boy, come on.' Everything now is slow and I am fading away to somewhere then I faintly hear someone calling, then it gets louder, and now someone is shaking me, 'NED, COMO'N NED, I'm NOT LOSING YOU NED KELLY.'

Suddenly me head sort of clears and I am no longer floating but I am me again, and it's the good Doctor Nicholson that has saved me, and he is still shaking me when he realizes that I am back. 'Thank God,' he exclaims and sinks into a chair.

CHAPTER TWENTY FOUR

My Country No More

I do not know how long I was in another place, or half dead, but I am feeling more like meself and when Superintendent Sadleir comes to me and says "Welcome back Ned,' I knows I must have been near death. 'Are you up to seeing your sister again?' I tells Superintendent Sadleir that I am ready, and in runs Maggie. 'Ned,' she cries, 'they said you had died.'

Grace, me little sister now pushes past Sadleir, who is standing just inside the doorway, and as Grace joins Maggie in hugging me near back to death, Dr Nicholson, says that they can only stay two minutes, and he ushers everyone away from the door which he shuts despite an objection from Sadleir.

The good Doctor then sits in the far corner to give us a little privacy, and me sisters settle down a bit as I ask what has been happening at the Inn. Maggie does most of the talking telling me that after they left me before they went down to near the Inn which was being fired upon from all directions, and one of the officers with a very loud voice yelled for em to stop shooting, then said to the remaining people inside that they have ten minutes to come out. Well they came out alright with their hands up, and we were all watching and hoping that the police would not open fire on them like before.

Maggie says Tom Lloyd walked up to Superintendent Sadleir as the people were coming out and said quietly but firmly, 'if even one of your men fires upon these innocent people, then believe me Sadleir we have many armed men here as you have seen, and the wrath of them will be more than any, or all your murdering traps could possibly handle.'

Superintendent Sadleir knows there are about eighty armed sympathisers over near the McDonnell Inn, so Maggie tells me he takes Tom's warning seriously and yells for his officers to hold their fire. 'Do not shoot,' Sadleir keeps yelling as about thirty people make their way towards him. Maggie goes on to say that Tom Lloyd went back to the waiting sympathisers and watched, but no police fired until all those who were willing to come out had done so. 'Then,' Maggie says, ' someone inside the Inn, or it may have been a trap on the other side of the Inn, fires a shot and next thing all the traps are thinking Dan, Steve and Joe are still in there and it's them firing, so the traps start firing again.'

Grace now tells me that Maggie is approached by Constable John Kelly, who is no relation, and he asks her if she would go to the Inn to talk to her brother and the others and get them to come out. Grace tells me that Maggie tells him that she would rather see them 'burn' first. This is what did happen, Grace goes on to tell me. She says that Kate was about to go to call out at the Inn when someone yells that the place is on fire. Grace tells how the fire takes hold quickly and it is obvious that anyone inside could not survive.

Maggie takes over the story again and she tells me that Father Gibney walks up to Superintendent Sadleir and tells him that he is going to enter the burning Inn to see if he could save some lives. But Sadleir tells the priest that he would not allow It. 'Ned if you could have heard this wonderful human tell this Superintendent of police a thing or two.' Maggie tells me that Father Gibney says to Sadleir, 'do you think Superintendent, that you can use the same method of standover tactics with me as you have used against these people. You're so called 'law officers' have killed innocent people here, and as I speak they are still firing wildly. Then, not satisfied with murdering the innocent in your plight to settle with the Kelly Gang, you have set fire to this very building. No Superintendent this is not me speaking, but the wrath of "God." So step aside and let me see if I can save some lives.'

Maggie says that there were about a thousand onlookers and most cheered this fine Father Gibney loudly as he walked through smoke and flames into The Glenrowan Inn. She tells me it was as if some "force" took control of these previously overzealous traps and not one of em fired a shot. Not even the traps around the other side. Maggie says then they finally noticed that no one is firing from

THE SPIRIT OF NED

inside the Inn. She said a hush of silence is held by everyone for several minutes, then with hands held high cause he has seen only too well how trigger happy the traps are, Father Gibney comes out of the burning building. 'They are all dead,' Maggie says the priest told everybody.

Grace now remembers something and tells me that Thomas Dixon must have gone in the back way cause he comes out carrying old Martin Cherry who was alive but died not long after. Doctor Nicholson now gets up and tells me sisters that their time is up, but I have one more visitor. Maggie and Grace says goodbye to me and Wild Wright comes in and quickly says to me that there has been trouble with the traps over the two bodies who they believe are Dan and Steve. I asks him what sort of trouble, and he tells me that Joe's body was taken out before the roof fell in and it was recognizable but the other two were burnt so badly they could not be certain that they were Dan and Steve, and at first the traps said we could take these two bodies and bury them.

Wild Wright goes on to tell me that as they were taking these bodies away, one of the Superintendents and a dozen armed traps 'tries to stop us, so we, about a hundred of us, challenges em and Tom tells em that if they do try to stop us then they will have to fight us.' Smiling now Wild Wright says, 'they backed down Ned.'

Wild Wright is excited now as he says to me, 'Ned we are still with you. Say the word and we will break you out of here. We are enough to beat them Ned.' I looks at this man that I had to fight many years ago, and I tells him, 'it's over. Go back to Tom and tell him and all the men that I Ned Kelly wants em all to give it away.

Look at me Wild me friend, and tell me truthfully, do you want all of you to finish up like this. Near dead I am. No, it's over, me brother is safe and can start a new life, go home to your families and help build a better Australia. We have got the attention of at least all of Australia, and the public, I'm sure will force a change in the way our country is governed and the way the Police are using standover tactics on the poor battlers but let the rich get away with anything. Tell Tom and everyone that I thanks em one and all. Tell em that Ned Kelly wants em to better themselves and help make this country great. Think not now of revolution, help make this country a real Australia by becoming a republic.'

I am not sure what I am saying or if I am saying anything as I feel sort of light headed and almost far away. But this clears and I realize Wild Wright is still here. Then I see something I never thought I would ever see. This man before me, once called the toughest man in Victoria, the former bare-knuckle champion, lays his big hand on me shoulder and he cries like a baby. I breaks his mood by asking him what happened to Joe Byrne's body, and he tells me that the traps have taken it away on a train. There is much noise outside the door of this office that has served as me hospital, and then in comes Sadleir, who tells Wild Wright that his visit is over. Wild Wright looks at me, hopefully, but I shakes me head, and he leaves. And so do I.

Apparently Superintendent Sadleir had been told by his superior, Standish, that it may not be safe to keep me here. They must have thought that the sympathisers might indeed break me out.

When I can see that they are ready to shift me, I gives me "sash" to Doctor Nicholson and tells him that they won't let me keep it where they are taking me and that I would like him to have it in a way of thanks for looking after me. It were very hard to part with that "sash" but I figured the good Doctor would look after it. 'Thank you Ned,' I am told, and I wonder if he or anyone ever notices that there is a little piece missing from one corner. I know that Dan, me Brother has this little piece.

So I am loaded on to a train, mattress and all very quickly and am on me way to Benalla. I know I am leaving this country, "my country." But it is "my country" no more.

CHAPTER TWENTY FIVE

I Am Still Ned

I sleep or am semi-conscious and next thing I am locked in a cell in the Benalla Gaol. As soon as the two guards, Constables Ryan and Kelly notice that I am stirring, in they come and they can't resist this opportunity to hassle me. They quiz me and ask many questions that I don't answer. Then the trap who escaped at Stringybark Creek, Constable McIntyre comes in to me cell and is much better mannered than the others.

McIntyre asks me in front of witnesses if he had shown any cowardice at Stringybark Creek. 'Why do you ask me that?' I figure the nervous Constable obviously want to clear any stigma from his record, and he says, 'I ask you because you are Ned Kelly, and everyone knows your word is good.' So I am still "Ned Kelly" and this trap values me opinion. I thinks for a while then I says loud enough for all to hear, 'Do I think you are a coward McIntyre?' I makes em all wait for me answer, then I says, 'No;'

The lot of em then leave me alone, but as they are leaving I hears Constable Ryan say, 'He's still Ned Kelly.' I am feeling quite weak and tired so I sleeps all night, and in the morning they carts me even further from "my country."

It is one of the officers who tells me this very morning, the twenty ninth day of June in the year eighteen eighty that it's to Melbourne they are taking me. When we gets there I looks and sees Superintendent Hare, the big trap that led the first attack on the Glenrowan Inn, a few days ago, and I sees his hand bandaged where I shot him. I now realise I am not yet in Melbourne but some other station and me mind is all mixed up, but again I looks across at Hare and glare at this mongrel who has hounded me family for years, but he cannot hold me eye and looks away.

Then to me great pleasure, coming towards me is this sweet young girl with black hair flowing. I have courted her on more than one occasion, and am happy to see her. No one tries to stop her and she comes and holds me close and cries. Then we must part and I am now in the guards van of a train, and this time on me way to Melbourne.

A new Doctor, named Charles Ryan is to look after me and also in with me is Magistrate Alfred Wyatt, who is highly thought of and respected by the good people. Magistrate Wyatt tells me he has offered his time to come with me to make sure the law is upheld in the treatment of me from now on. I asks him why he has done such a good deed and he tells me that he believes that the police may have overstepped the mark in their treatment of us Kelly's. This good man also tells me that when he heard that the police were going to string up the body of Joe Byrne and let the photographers loose, he tried to stop them. I thanked him and he goes on to tell me that there was a near riot as the hundreds of people yelled at the police to let Joe's body down and to give him a proper burial.

Magistrate Wyatt keeps talking to me and tells me he is not happy with the actions of the police, not only against me family and the other people, particularly the way that they have fired upon and killed innocent people.

He says he will do his best to hold a royal commission into the whole affair right from the start of the disgraceful way me mother was locked up. 'You Ned will suffer,' he says. 'But you will be remembered for standing up to these dictators who I assure you will be brought to justice and a new level of law makers will follow in this country. Unfortunately you Ned may not see these changes but you have made your mark, and you WILL be remembered.'

I am now pleased that I stopped the sympathisers from any further shooting at Glenrowan. I was about to say thank you again to this honest and fair Magistrate when I falls into a coma, and can only faintly remember things after that, but I must have been dreaming cause I thought I could hear someone keep calling "You ARE Ned Kelly."

CHAPTER TWENTY SIX

Pentridge Again

The next person I remembers seeing is the Governor of this dreaded Pentridge gaol where I was falsely locked up so many years ago. He is signing the papers to put me in his legal care. This self-important man directs the warders to take me to the prison hospital, where a Doctor Shields is to look after me. Guards are everywhere and I thinks why do they need so many to watch a near dead, trussed up person who could have no chance of escaping anyway.

I smile at this next person who is a priest who tells me his name is Father Aylward and that he is a friend of Father Gibney who gave the "last Rites" to me at Glenrowan. 'From what Father Gibney tells me Ned, you are lucky to be with us still. Maybe someone special is looking after you my son,' he says. I thank him and say I would be pleased if he could pray with me. Father Aylward does pray with me and for me for about an hour, then he tells me that he now going to visit me mother, and wants to know if I have any messages for her, or if I have any news for her. I asks him what news he already had to tell her and he says that he has been told that I was the only survivor, and that I was near death.

I ponders for a moment then ask him to give me love to Ma and tell her I am sorry, and that I have kept me promise. I am still not over me loss of so much blood so I sleep a lot and time moves quickly. Then on the second day I think is, I asks a guard what day it is and he tells me it is the Thirtieth Day of June Eighteen

Eighty, and this turned out to be a good day for me. Are these very eyes of mine playing tricks? Am I in a coma, or maybe I am dreaming, for there coming closer is me Ma whom I have not seen for over two years.

But this is not the vibrant full of life lady that she was when they took her away to serve time in this rotten place. But Ma must be all of forty eight now, and as she gets near me I can see how pale she has become. 'Neddie me boy,' and me spell is broken. This is me Ma, and as she showers me with hugs and kisses, I says to her, 'Ma I am sorry.' She cries a bit, then says, 'what about Dan?' I tells her that we all fought bravely.' Then I looks her straight in her eyes and tell her I made a promise to her about Dan and I kept me promise.

Ma smiles knowingly at me, and as the guards are listening we say no more about me brother in case they work out that Dan is indeed alive. We do talk as mother and son for a half hour or so and I tells her as best I can all that has happened, but time goes too fast and the guards move to take me beloved Ma away and our visit is over.

The month of July goes and me health improves. August it now and I am taken for me committal hearing to Beechworth. Constable Bracken was in the group of several Police escorting me. Bracken looks quizzingly at me when, as we pass through Glenrowan I says, 'a good man had fallen there.' He, Bracken, does not know that Dan and Steve escaped, so he probably was wondering why I did not say 'three good men' instead of 'a good man.'

There were about two hundred traps guarding me and the courthouse, and I was so surrounded by them I could not see any of me family or friends amongst the big crowd of onlookers. I could not walk properly yet, and could not stand for long. I am not allowed visitors but unbeknown to me, Maggie and Tom Lloyd had been to Melbourne to obtain the legal services of a Mr David Gaunson to who I was granted a few minutes with to prepare me defence at this trial, which was a farce, and I was remanded stand trial in October.

As I was being led away, and before the guards realized it, Maggie and Tom rushes forward and shakes me hand, then me other sister Kate kisses me. Then in that brief moment I received a kiss on me hand from this pretty young lady who I had been seeing. The Police Guards then quickly ushered me away.

Back to Pentridge I am taken again, with the knowledge that I am remanded for trial on the Twenty Eighth of October in the Melbourne Criminal Court. Time now drags and I am getting healthier, but still no visitors except for Father Alyward who comes regularly, and brings me any newspaper bits that he thinks I might like, or are about The Kelly Gang. One story in the Ovens and Murray Advertiser tells how the feeling amongst the people is that the police were greatly to blame for the debacle at Mrs Jones's Inn at Glenrowan. It goes on to say that the Government is to hold a "Royal Commission," and an inquiry into the organization of the police force.

Another story from the Argus asks the question as to why the police were allowed to fire into the Inn when they knew there were women and children inside. It puts to the readers the question of who lit the fire. This good Father Alyward also visits Ma and passes messages to and fro for us, and he tells me that when Ma got back to her cell after visiting me, that Governor Castieau was there, so she asked him if she could again be permitted to visit me and he told Ma that she will be allowed to see me before me execution. This must have upset Ma as she told Father Alyward that she was afraid that I might try to take me own life.

Because I am getting no visitors, and I know that it is because the establishment won't allow em to come, I writes this letter,

To,

The Honourable,

The Chief Secretary

'Sir,

I beg most respectfully to request your permission to send for me sister, Mrs Skillion to visit me at the hospital of this gaol, to enable me to confer with her respecting the provision of a solicitor to prepare me defence at me forthcoming trial and likewise to provide me with the necessary clothing to appear there at. I would also like you to allow me to see me mother. I have only seen her once.

Your obedient servant,

Edward Kelly.'

I writes this letter hoping to get a written reply, but all I got was a verbal one from a guard saying they were looking into it. I now held no hope or visions of me ever leaving this place, at least not alive.

I do have visions though. I can "see" me Ma free to go back to her little farm and all the family. I have a "vision" of me brother living on to a ripe old age and getting married and having a daughter, but his name in me "vision" was not Dan Kelly. But I can "see" him working with his horses that he loves so much.

These visions or dreams, I believe come to me as a message or indication to me that me life may be shortened, but me loved ones can and will live on. A man who is used to freedom and living in the bush thinks differently and sometimes dreams a bit. I dreams that this country will one day be free of the standover type Government and would truly become a free and Democratic Nation. I dream of the poor and down trodden being equal and given a chance, and I not only dream but hope that the indigenous Australians will be treated as equal and not be pushed around and even murdered because they are in the way of the rich who truly believe that they are better than these people.

I even, God forgive me, hope and dream that my rebellious actions against these oppressors will help to start the chance of equal rights for all in our country.

Yes I dare to dream these things, and I do have a "vision" that we all can say together, with pride, 'we are Australians.' I thinks that there may be some hope of this starting to happen, cause just recently Peter Lalor who stood up to the tyranny at the Eureka Stockade, has been selected as speaker at Parliament.

Still I am not allowed visitors, and am transferred to a solitary confinement cell, and as I look around this tiny cell, I reads on a wall, "Innocent until proven Irish." I start to laugh at this message scratched into the concrete, then I stops laughing, cause I realize it is true.

CHAPTER TWENTY SEVEN

Trial or Event?

Henry Bindoon, I finds out is to defend me, as there in no money to employ a good defence lawyer. The man we wanted was David Guanson but his fee of fifty guineas for two days was beyond our reach, or more so beyond Maggie's reach, as she was doing her best to handle things.

I had no money as I had given Dan and Steve a hundred quid each to make good their getaway, and I had stashed another two hundred quid in a secret location that only Tom Lloyd and Maggie knows about, and where it is hidden. This two hundred is for Ma after she gets out of gaol, and there is no way I am going to use that money for me defence which will only be an event put on to make it look like they gave me a trial.

I knows that they will have a chosen jury and that they will have Judge Barry presiding over it and the result will be. I stop thinking about it, and get meself ready for the event, and I am taken early and everyone involved is also early, except for Hanging Barry who is late, and I knows he is building up his self-importance and is going to make a good show of this, his day of glory. Yes, thinks I this will not be a trial as such but an event that they the dictators will try to glorify for their own egos.

Finally Judge Barry swaggers into the packed courtroom and after the usual opening acts, my inexperienced lawyer, Mr Bindoon, asks for an adjournment on the grounds that he has not had time to familiarise himself with the facts of the case. Even I found this comical and of course it was denied. What chance have I?

Me defence lawyer has given up after ten minutes, and this is the man who is supposed to be saving me very life.

The court is asked, 'how does Edward Kelly plead?' Looking straight at Barry, the mongrel who locked me Ma away on the evidence of a lying police Constable Fitzpatrick, who was later sacked for perjury and drunkenness as well as failing to do his duty as a police officer, I says, 'Not Guilty.'

If I before thought I had any chance, I now feel I have not a hope in hell cause the first prosecution witness is Constable McIntyre, and he has clearly been told what to say and he perjures hisself by giving a different story to what he gave at me inquest at Beechworth about Stringybark Creek.

Today he lies and says Lonigan showed no sign of going for his gun, whilst at Beechworth he had told the truth saying that Lonigan had drawn his gun and was aiming me. I knows I am wasting me time but I stands up and gives a sign that he is lying. McIntyre cannot look at me at first, but when he does glance me way I cannot resist mouthing to him, 'you ARE a coward.' The day goes with no progress, and they adjourn proceedings till the morrow.

The second day goes no better for me, especially as they allow no witness for me, and Bindoon just sits there. Maggie, Tom Lloyd and Kate are in the front row, and don't look happy with proceedings. Bindoon did at least try to get me Jerilderie letter read out but it was not allowed. Sergeant Steele is called and sure enough, this man that intentionally shot women and children, carries on the lies, saying that 'Ned Kelly told him that he had shot Constable Fitzpatrick with the intention of killing the police officer.' When the tyranny and dictatorship sinks as low as letting police officers lie and perjure themselves, and their evidence is taken notice of, then not only have I no hope, but this country has no hope or future.

I dares to dream that Magistrate Wyatt can get a 'Royal Commission' into this corrupt Victorian Police Force. If me being the scape goat to bring forth this corruption to the public, then some good may come of this whole affair, including me Ma's unjust gaoling.

CHAPTER TWENTY EIGHT

"May the Lord Have Mercy on Your Soul."

The trial is over before too much longer and me lawyer still has done not a thing.

So I watch as this now smirking Judge Sir Redmond Barry, now asks the "selected" jury for their verdict. I wonders why he bothers to ask em when he has already told em that they must find me guilty.

'Guilty,' says Samuel Lazarus in his strong Liverpool accent.

You could hear a pin drop as the clerk of courts asks if the prisoner has anything to say.

I stands up and bows to the assembly, glares at the Judge and Jury which contained at least one former policeman, then I says, 'Well it's rather too late for me to speak now. I asked to be allowed to speak when it mattered and I was not permitted to do so then, so please don't try to make it look as though you have given me a fair trial, cause you have not.'

There is now an uproar in this very courthouse and the court crier has to call for silence. 'Edward Kelly,' starts Judge Barry, and he goes on about the jury and all the legal sayings, in his finest voice. Then he says many things about me, mostly to make himself appear important. I fires up when his arrogance goes too far by saying to me, 'your unfortunate and miserable companions have died a death, which probably you might envy, but you are not afforded the opportunity.'

'I don't think there is much proof that they did die the death,' I snaps back at him.

'I have now to pronounce your sentence.' The man known as the "Hanging Judge" pauses to get the right effects, and all is now silent as he continues, even though his face is now a glowing red. 'Prisoner at the bar, the sentence of this court is that you will be taken to a place from where you came, and you will be taken thence at such a time to such a place as his Excellency the Governor will direct, and you will be hanged by the neck until you are dead. May the lord have mercy upon your Soul.'

All is very quiet until I says back to him, 'I will go a little further than that and say I will see you there, where I go.'

'Remove the prisoner,' says Judge Barry. The warders move forward but I signal them to stop and I turn to me sisters and blows them a kiss and says, 'Goodbye.'

I am led away and as I pass me defence lawyer Henry Bindoon, I shakes me head, and I see that he is a useless broken man, near crying in self-pity. Now I am changed into prison clothes and have "Irons" riveted around me legs so I cannot walk or run through me concrete walls or me metal door of me tiny cell. There are guards at me door twenty four hours a day and they watch to make sure I don't grow wings and fly out of here, anyway they never take their eyes off me.

A few day of only having Father Alyward to talk to, I happily receive some welcome visitors, and as I hoped it is Maggie and Tom and Kate, also with them are some friends, the McAuliffe's Dennis and his Sister Margaret and Joe Ryan. They are allowed to stay for quite a time and we talk about old times and Tom Lloyd say that they are taking up a petition, and there will be an appeal that William Gaunson, the Brother of me former attorney is going to donate his time to, as he is appalled at the way me trial was handled. Tom Lloyd tells me that the reason I am allowed visitors is cause William who is a member of the Society for the Abolition of Capital Punishment, had a meeting with the Premier Sir Graham Berry.

I thanks him, but I don't hold any great hopes. I asks Maggie if she has any special news, and she understands that I mean about Dan, and she gives me a nod and a smile, but I know she can't say much as the guards are listening. Maggie

THE SPIRIT OF NED

tells me that she is going to try to get me more visits, and hopefully Ma will be allowed to come soon. It's time for them to go, and Kate, then Maggie give me a hug, then Tom shakes me hand and then looks me squarely in the eye and tells me that he will look after the family.

Maggie now comes back just as the guard is letting them all out, and he is out of earshot for a brief second, so me sister says 'we got word that Dan is away and he sends his all to you, and Ned I am going to have a baby in about six months, and Tom and I want your blessing by allowing us to, if it is a boy, to name him Ned.' I hugs me sister tightly and she is gone. This message picked me up and I was happily humming out the tune of Danny Boy when I felt something tickling inside me shirt, so I fishes it out casually so the guard can't see and glory be it's the piece of me very own sash that I had cut off and given to Dan to get back to me when he is safely away. Maggie, God bless her, must have slipped it inside me very shirt when she was giving me a hug. Good news it was that Maggie was pregnant, and they had chosen me name if the child was a boy.

Well I am that pleased that I must have been smiling cause the guard, a surely bugger at the best of times, says, 'and what have you got to smile at then Kelly?' I am so pleased that me brother is safe to live on, and Maggie is to have a child to Tom Lloyd that I amuses me self a little by saying to this guard who thinks I am too happy, 'Oh Mr Warder, have you not heard the news that I am to be hung?'

This makes him think and he tells me that of course he has heard, but he asks me how come this makes me smile. I give him me best smile and say, 'Cause then I won't have to see your surely face anymore.'

CHAPTER TWENTY NINE

Me Last Days

I longed for a visit from Ma, I did so badly want to see her one more time. The good Father O'Hea surprises me a few days later, and we pray together, then he tells me he has visited me Ma and she is holding up well. He also tells me he is making sure that she is allowed to visit me. Father O'Hea listens as I say a prayer that I have just written,

'Why me Lord?
What have I ever done?
That deserves even one,
Of the pleasures I've known.
What did I ever do?
That deserves loving you,
And the forgiveness you've shown.'

Father O'Hea leans over and as he can now see the words, he joins in with me,

So help me Jesus,
I'm needing you, so help me Jesus,
I know what I am.
Lord help me Jesus,
Jesus, my souls in your hands.'

Exercise helps me through these times, although it is hard with these leg irons on. Time itself goes slow and I find meself remembering or sort of reliving some of me past. One thing comes to me quickly, probably cause of the news from Maggie about Dan, I thinks back how we The Kelly Gang spoke of breaking up one day and going far away to start new lives, and around the campfire we each put forward the name we may use if we did this. I cannot remember the name I chose and it does not matter now for me, and Joe Byrne would not put forward a name cause he reckoned that he was a dead man, and poor Joe, he was right.

Steve Hart was adamant that he would be called Fred Layton. Me Brother Dan kept changing his choices. Some of Dan's choices I remember are hard to remember but one that sticks in me mind is Jack, Jack O'Day, or Jack Day. Then as I'm thinking about this I recall how later Joe comes up with Joe Knight because he always wanted to be a 'knight,' besides he did say that we all would look like 'knights' in our armour.

When next father O'Hea comes, he tells me that a petition has been signed by thirty two thousand people asking for a reprieve for me life. We pray and he says if it comes to the worst he promises to be with me. I thanks him and tell this man who some twenty five years ago did christen me, that it will mean a lot to me to have him there at me end. Governor Castieau comes to me on Melbourne Cup day and he tells me that he had a shilling each way on a horse called Grand Flanner at six to one. I think he was waiting for me to ask him if it won, but I did not give him that pleasure. Instead I asks him if he has any news for me.

Castieau promptly snaps that the petition has been declined and the date for me hanging has been set for the eleventh of this month, November, and he walks out. So it is, I says to meself, nine days left on this very earth. I starts to dream a lot more, and I dream that if I was ever going to settle down it may well have been with that black haired young lady who came to see me when I was being transferred from Glenrowan to here. I dreams about me Ma, then I do me temper and kick the hell out of me "leg irons," which does not do me legs a lot of good. I reckon that now I'm a goner, if I could turn back the clock I surely would go after that rotten Fitzpatrick, who was responsible for all of this.

Sometimes now I imagine I can hear me Ma singing as she used to. To pass the time I hum out lots of old songs, and one night I am humming the tune, "In the sweet bye and bye," and I know the Warder is close and is listening, when I'll be blowed if he don't start singing as I hum. I stops and then sing with him for a while, then he gives me a smoke. We talks for a while and he says that most people he knows feel that Ned Kelly has been badly done by.

After he goes back to his chair outside me cell where he is supposed to write down anything I say or do, I continue humming and singing, and when I starts singing "Danny Boy" I automatically feel for the little piece of me "sash" which I had given to me Brother Dan, and he sent it back to me when he was away and safe, so I knew he was alright.

CHAPTER THIRTY

Such Is Life

The next several days I receive no visitors, but most of the guards are friendlier now and tell me news and talk to me more. One tells me that several thousand people had demonstrated through the streets of Melbourne demanding that my reprieve be made law, he tells me that the crowd was joined by many more and they marched to parliament house or somewhere and demonstrated.

Each day I would ask to see the governor cause I wanted him to allow Ma to visit me, but I had to wait until the day before me hanging was to take place before he comes. I treats him with all respect, and asks him, 'Please Governor, could I have me mother to see me and could I have a photograph taken for her to keep. Early that afternoon of the tenth day of November eighteen eighty, I am taken out to the "yard" to have me picture taken, then I am led, like a dog on a leash, back to me cell. I have some spare moments to think, and the letter that I dictated to David Gaunson several days ago comes into me mind. Me idea in presenting this letter to the public was probably to make it clear that I had a conscience, and I know that I have done wrong, but I sure believe I have been hounded. I dictated this, "I do not pretend that I have led a blameless life, or that one fault justified another, but the public judging a case like mine should remember, that the darkest life may have a bright side, and that after the worst has been said against a man, he may, if he is heard, tell a story in his own rough way, that will perhaps lead them to intimate the harshness of their thoughts against him, and find as many excuses for him as he would plead for himself." I writes more and David Gaunson gets me to sign it.

Soon after getting back, Ma is led into me cell and we embrace and tell each other that we loves the each of us. I tells Ma that they have taken pictures of me and she will get one. 'Our people will not forget you Ned.'

Ma is now crying, and I cannot keep me eyes dry. The guards come and Ma is going to leave me for the last time. We hug and I looks at me Ma, holding her image in me brain, and I say, 'Goodbye me Mother.'

Ma says 'Goodbye Neddie,' and turns to go, then she stops, turns to me and says, 'Mind you die like a Kelly son.'

Not long afterwards me Brother Jim, and me Sisters Kate and Grace comes to me. This was also only a short visit, during which I asked after Maggie, and Kate tells me through sobs, that dear Maggie could not bear it anymore, but to tell you goodbye from her. I asks Kate to tell Maggie that I loves her, and thanks her for all she has done.

This visit is over and amid all the tears and hugs me brother and sisters go, but I am not alone for long, as Governor Castieau brings his son to see Ned Kelly. Not too long later in comes Tom Lloyd and his sister Kate and we hug and before we say our goodbyes I reminds Tom the hiding place of the "saddle" I had hidden for Ma when she gets out. I tell Tom that if I had lived on I would have been proud to have him as a brother in law.

He nods and tells me that he already thinks of me as a brother. He promises to look after me Sister Maggie as long as he lives. We shake hands, then Tom Lloyd, me friend and partner of me dear sister Maggie tells me something that I already knows. He tells me how they want to name their first boy after me. Tom has kept his composure up to now, but I am now looking at a big strong man with tears rolling down his face, and he mumbles 'strength to you Ned.'

Kate, Tom's younger sister comes to me now and kisses me full on the mouth. She is sobbing uncontrollably and cannot talk. Tom has to drag her away, and they are gone.

Alone I am, and the knowledge that I will never see any of me family or loved ones ever again now hits me. Me mood is broken by the chief gaol cook, and he tells me that I can order whatever I like for dinner, so I does.

That night me last night on earth I enjoys what me Ma would have cooked for me. I am given roast lamb, peas, potatoes and gravy. This fine meal I washes down with a bottle of wine which was delivered with me dinner.

Everything is hazy after that last night, but I gets up early, does me stretches and then prays a lot, and before I know they take me leg irons off and the prison Chaplain, Father Donaghy takes me confession. Then an escorted walk to the condemned cell.

During this walk me mind is saying 'Yea though I walk through the valley of the shadow of death, I shall fear no evil, for thou art with me.' We are soon in this cell and in comes, as he promised he would, Father O'Hea. Both Fathers gives me the last rites. Then it is time. I looks to Father O'Hea, and after a long moment, he blesses me and says, 'have strength, and show courage Ned.'

Now is me last short walk and before I realize it they are ready to cover me head. I Feel for and find comfort in the little piece of me sash, then I says 'so it has come to this.'

The rope which I would not look at, I now feels around me neck, and then I somehow think I can see me Dad, and then Ma, and can almost hear me Brothers and Sisters all at once. Then I am sure I can hear Dan's voice singing "Danny boy".

I now feel stronger and I hum along with Dan's voice in me head. Then, I hear me own voice say,

'Such is life.'

BIBLIOGRAPHY

Chapters 6,8,12, and 30.
Song: Danny Boy, 1976 singer Elvis Presley R C A
Written by Frederick Weatherly all rights reserved by
BMG Music.

Chapter 11
Song: the Black Velvet Band sung by THE DUBLINERS
1968 EMI Records
First aired about 1842 as The Girl with the Black Velvet Band.

Chapter 18
Song: The Wild Colonial Boy sung by Trad. Firr: The Wooden Spoon
1992 Hughes leisure Group Mona Vale Sydney Australia.
The origins of this Song are obscure according to The All Australian Song Book
By Patrick Cook. Angus and Robertson Publishers 0 207 147558 1984

Chapter 21
Song: Why Me (Lord) singer, writer,
Kris Kristofferson, 1990, CBS Records Inc.

Chapter 30
Letter dictated to David Gaunson,
At Her Majesty's Gaol, Melbourne.
1 November 1880.
Signed, Edward Kelly.

www.ingramcontent.com/pod-product-compliance
Lightning Source LLC
Chambersburg PA
CBHW072049290426
44110CB00014B/1616